UNBREAKABLE
THE RISE, THE FIRE, AND THE FIGHT

Councilmember
Tiawana Brown
"The People's Champ
When We Fight, We Win"

TIAWANA BROWN

© 2025 by Tiawana Brown

All rights reserved. No part of this book may be reproduced, stored in a retrieval system or transmitted in any form or by any means without the prior written permission of the publishers, except by a reviewer who may quote brief passages in a review to be printed in a newspaper, magazine or journal.

All rights reserved.

ISBN: 978-1-953760-49-4
Pure Thoughts Publishing, LLC. Conyers, GA 30013
www.purethoughtspublishing.com
Printed in the United States of America.

Table of Contents

Dedications v

Acknowledgments ix

THE RISE 1

   Introduction: Why I'm Writing This Now..................................3

   Interlude: The Women Who Raised Me 9

   Chapter 1: Southside Housing Project: Humble Beginnings 15

      The Foundation That Built Me..16

      My Mama's Walk..17

      Life in Southside Homes..19

   Chapter 2: The Streets, the Cheerleader, and the First Hit..........22

   Chapter 3: A Box Checked 28

   Chapter 4: The Fast Life, The Fall, and The Faith 34

   Chapter 5: The Ride to Alderson..38

   Chapter 6: The First Day Inside Alderson 42

   Chapter 7: The Birth Inside the Walls 47

   Chapter 8: The Healing Begins 51

   Chapter 9: Beauty After the Bars: The Movement 55

   Chapter 10: The Movement Continues 59

THE FIRE..**61**

   Chapter 11: From the Projects to The People's Champ................63

   Chapter 12: The Fire Inside City Hall 69

   Chapter 13: When the Fire Turned on Me 74

THE FIGHT..**83**

   Chapter 14: Faith, Family and; Forward 85

   Chapter 15: The Heartbeat of City Hall 89

   Closing Reflection 93

   Author's Reflection 94

   Epilogue 97

   About Author..99

Dedications

To My Daughters, Antoinette Rouse and Tijema Brown

You are my heart, my healing, and my forever "why."

We have walked through storms most people will never fully understand, yet here we are — still standing. You have carried me through moments that could have broken us, and instead we found a deeper strength born from love, truth, and unshakeable faith.

Antoinette, my calm in the chaos — your quiet power and grace steady me when the world feels heavy.

Tijema, my fire and twin flame — your courage, conviction, and fearless love remind me of the women we come from.

Together, you are my balance — the calm and the fire, the grace and the grit. You are my legacy walking, my love breathing, my proof that we can rise through rumor, pain, or persecution.

I dedicate this entire book — this fight and this freedom — to you both. Your mother didn't just survive. She refused to surrender. And so did you.

I love you endlessly.

— Mom

To My Mother, Artie Mae Brown

You are my beginning, my blueprint, and my first teacher in faith, strength, and survival.

From you, I learned how to stand tall when life tried to bend me. You showed me that love is not weakness — it is warfare wrapped in grace. Your hands built the woman I became, and your prayers carried me through every jail cell, every courtroom, and every council chamber.

When the world forgot who I was, you whispered my name back into purpose through prayer. Because of you, I lead with heart. Because of you, I know that strength can be soft and faith can be fierce.

I dedicate this journey to you, Mama. Your love made me unbreakable.

— Your daughter,
Tiawana

To My Sister, Chunta Olaseha

You are my anchor in every storm, my laughter in the middle of pain, and my reminder that family is who stands with you when the world feels heavy.

You have loved me through the fire, believed in me when others doubted, and carried me with prayers I didn't even know I needed. You never asked for credit — you just showed up, again and again, with the kind of love that holds, heals, and restores.

You know the woman behind the titles and the heart behind the headlines. You have never let me forget who I am, even when I almost did.

Every phone call, every text message- every moment- you have been right by my side. This victory belongs to you too. I love you beyond words. You became My Best friend from your birth and until infinity, and forever.

— Your sister,
Tiawana

To My Aunt Valarie Brown Gardner

You are the quiet strength behind so many of our stories. You never had biological children of your own, yet you helped raise all of us with love, discipline, and grace.

Your life — your education, your work, your marriage, your service, and now your leadership in the church — has been a living sermon on strength, integrity and faith. Your poems, your prayers, and your constant reminder to "pray and trust God" have carried me farther than you know.

Thank you for being our foundation, our quiet teacher, and our steady light.

With all my love,
— Tiawana

Acknowledgments

First, To God

To my God — You are everything, and everything is You. Thank You for Your grace and mercy, for never leaving me, and for loving me even when I could not love myself. Every victory, every lesson, and every breath of strength in this book belongs to You first.

My Family — The Browns, The Roots

To my mama, **Artie Mae Brown** — my heartbeat and my foundation. To my daughters, **Antoinette and Tijema**, and my grandson, **Byron Jr.** — you are my living proof that love and legacy endure.

To my sister **Chunta Olaseha**, her husband **Tommy Olaseha**, my nephew **Isaac**, and my niece Elizabeth aka **Lizzy** — the calls, the laughter, and the way you always answer when I need you remind me that sisters and family are God's gifts.

To **Aunt Valarie**, **Aunt Shirley**, and my cousin/aunt **Barbara Phillips** — your wisdom, care, and prayers have covered our entire family. To my angels in heaven — **Grandma Lula, Granddaddy JW, Uncle Jerry Red- Head Brown, Aunt Linda, Aunt Deborah** and so many other family members in Heaven — your legacy lives in every step I take.

To all my family on my daddy's side of the family and thank you to my daddy-**Larry H. Reid** for helping keep those ties strong — thank you for your love and support, even though we didn't grow up side by side. A special shout out to Shakenna Billings- and for the record- all of you are the best family and support ever-. My siblings Chevella Belk and Cedric Reid- I thank God for both of you.

To My Step Daddy- Robert "Chicken" Welch- thank you for producing all of my bonus sisters- especially Vashti "Pookie Neely, April Neely-and Mia "MeMe" Williams- sisters are heaven sent- and to you Robbin Neely- you will always be my favorite Girl.

To my cousin-sister Barbara **"Pee-Wee"** Brown, **John Brown, (Belinda)** and cousins **Monique Campbell, Monica and DeVane English-Christa Nail, Christian "CJ" Nail, The Cherry Family, Latavia Brown , Jorandale Brown, James Campbell Jr., Ahmad "AJ" Cunningham, Nylah Campbell,** *Peaches and James Campbell, Sr.* - *all of you make the family tree better and to the next generation of the younger family tree- keep God 1st the sky is only a view. I thank God for my family.*

To **Latavia Brown**, thank you for the extra love and support that you give to My mama and Bj- we love you.

Bonus Daughter, Mariah "Meme" Osborne — our bond was built over decades of love, trust, and shared life. You bring me joy and sunshine on my cloudiest days. I love you, always.

Dijya Gill — my God-daughter. It has been a true honor to be your God mama. I hold nothing but love for you, always.

Bonus Son, Byron B. Sadler — your presence is a living reminder of God's grace and mercy. You are loved.

Cousins Nene Reid, Kim Reid, Shponda Major, Twins- Ded and Sed Major(My Angel Heaven) & Chris Major- to all of the Reid's, Major's and Cassell's- not listed. Thank you for having my back and reminding me that family is the real deal.

To all my bonus daughters and sons, my nieces and nephews, and every relative whose name may not appear here but whose love has sustained me — please know: it was never a slip of the heart, only of the page. You are seen. You are deeply loved.

Faith, Churches, and Spiritual Covering

To my spiritual families — thank you for keeping me covered:

- **Greater Mt. Sinai Baptist Church** (Rev. Dr. Major A. Stewart) — my family church, my home, and my anchor. You stood publicly when others stayed silent. You reminded the city what real shepherding looks like.

- **GAP Church International** (Bishop Anthony & First Lady Harriett Jinwright) — my spiritual parents. Your wisdom, guidance, and covering have shaped my walk. Every prayer you have prayed for me has worked.

- **Fire and Ice Ministry** (Pastor Darrius Williams & Dr. Dana Cathey-Williams) — Thank you so much-your prayers before, during, and after every storm have never failed.

- **Spirit of the Word Church** (Bishop Walter & First Lady Denise Gwin) — your raw, truthful preaching and open doors helped me rise unapologetically. It started with you and I will never forget how you poured into me.

- **Next Level Ministries Charlotte-**Pastor Charles E. Jacobs and First Lady Jacobs.

- **Weeping Willow AME Zion-**Pastor & Rev. Henrico White

- **New Foundation Church International,** - To my cousins Pastor Sam & Dr. Rico Wagner

- **New Covenant Bibleway Church-**Pastor CM Beatty III, and First Lady Beatty.

- **New Bethlehem Baptist Church (Detroit)-**Pastor LoveJoy Johnson, II

- **New Hope Missionary Baptist Church-** Pastor , Dr. Quientrell Burrell

- **Mission Church of the Lord -** Bishop Raley, First Lady Raley, Pastor Mark Raley & Sabrina Raley.

- **New St. Paul Holiness Church-** Pastor Anthony Crowder Sr, and First Lady Yolanda Nichols Crowder

- -and every pastor, first lady, intercessor, and member who prayed for me by name — thank you.

You reminded me that the Church is not just a building — it is a living body that lifts, covers, and restores.

Colleagues, Friends & Sisters

To my **American Airlines and Piedmont Airlines family**, my **iQor family**, and coworkers who turned into lifelong friends — thank you for every check-in, prayer, and hug. Being in aviation and customer care with you added a joy to my life I will always cherish.

To **my mentees — Lydia Avoki, Trinity Snowten, and Harmoni Moorer,** *Monae Brown and Shameka Dade—* you are the reason Beauty after the Bars exist- you are the "why." You prove daily that the system did not win. You did. I love all of you. Keep pushing, Keep going, Keep winning. Keep praying. Keep fighting. Never quit chasing your dreams.

Childhood and Lifetime-Friends - Forever in my Heart- You are my sisters girls- so you should know who you are!!!

To my circle of sisters — too many to list without missing someone — thank you for the calls, the texts, the kitchen-table talks, the "you got this" messages, the court appearances, the prayers, and the "I'm on my way" moments. You know who you are. On days when I wanted to throw in the towel, you snatched it back and handed it to me folded.

Thank you for standing with me during the Campaign – 2023-2025

Akya Canada, Amy Parker, Angela Huntley, Attorney Alesha Brown, Anna London, Aunt Patricia Love, Barry Barrett, Betty Dean Baker, Brandon & Judy Brown, Bobby Drakeford, Candy Sturdivant, Carlenia Ivory, Cedric Dean, Cedrice "NuffCed (The Ultimate Host) Brown, Celeste Wells, Charles Osborne, Cleesa Osborne (Marvin), Charlene Henderson, Colette Forrest, Colin Brown, Congresswoman Alma Adams, County Commissioner Mark Jerrell, D'Andrea K. Ely, Daniel, Danielle Metz, Dee Rainer, Donielle Prophete, Dr. Blanche Penn, Edie Blake, Elliott Vinson, Emma Allen, Evelyn Poe, Evelyn Hill aka Eve,

Former Councilmember & Mayor Pro Tem – Braxton Winston, Golden Quinn, Garrick Richardson, Jennifer Peas, Jessica A. Hollis- Summers, John C. Barnett, John Carmichael, Jordan Lopez, Kass Ottley, Keeda Haynes, Kendrick Cunningham, Kim Robinson, Kristie Puckett, Lucille Puckett, Lakertisha Slade-Mciver, Larry "No limit" Mims, Lakeisha Mobley, David & Mary Howard, Regina Walker Lawhorne, D' Marria Monday, Jennifer Sloan, Marcus Massey, Meko McCarthy, My spiritual Parents – Bishop Anthony Jinwright & First Lady Harriet Jinwright, Nicole Coco Davis (Thomas), Nerika Chocolate Jenkins, Pastor Darrius and Dr. Dana Williams, Pastor Gloria Smith, Rev. Dr. Janet Garner-Mullins, Ricky Hall, Rita Gray, Rodney McGill, Shamaiye Haynes, Sheriff Garry L. McFadden, Gemini Boyd, Shelby Jones, Sharon "Sha" Turner, Richard Kalmick, Richard DeShields (DBO DIVAS), Sheila Stevenson, Cemeka Mitchem Students at JCSU, Professor Jasmine Corbett and Janelle Stowe, Patrice Brown, Stephanie Sneed, Sylvia Horton, Tamara Dunham, Tawanda Johnson, Tracy Elkins, Tracey Robins, Toki Brome, Tonya Johnson- Oni, Terese-Swan Hutchinson, Tracy Siplin, Tray "Rock" Johns, Trunza Davis, Tyra Imani Patterson, Wanda Johnson, Wykisha Currie, Yolanda Besler & Tone-X

County Commissioner Arthur Griffin, wife Alicia Griffin & Daughter Christina Griffin- Thank you so much.

Everyone that donated to my campaign and voted for me- you are a part of History. All Volunteers- if I missed your name- you are not forgotten.

The Charlotte Airport Workers, and the Unions and especially SEIU.

My make-up artist- Da'Shanae Shariff- @letmypeoplefree- book cover #MUA and weekly artist for council meetings, and media appearances and speaking engagements. I love you niece- thank you for enhancing my beauty.

MUA- @facingparisb. - thank you for your service and making me feel beautiful. You are amazing. Love you.

Cover Photo Credit- Marcel Anthony, Tiana @ibanghair- Hair

Movement, Advocacy, and Justice

To the organizations and leaders who shaped my advocacy and amplified my voice:

- **National Council for Incarcerated and Formerly Incarcerated Women and Girls** — to Andrea James and the entire leadership and Board Members- Ari, Justine, Virginia, Big Shay- Danielle Metz, and all of the fierce sisters that I met in this movement-thank you for teaching me how to stand and fight for what is right, and for giving me a national sisterhood Globally.

- **JLUSA / JustLeadershipUSA**, Deanna Hoskins, Ronald Simpson-Bey and Staff- thank you for the investment in my bold leadership. It allows me to Lead with Conviction.

- **ANWOL (Susan Burton)**, - thank you for giving me a place to stand so that could change so many lives- your financial investment in Beauty after the Bars- is greatly appreciated.

- To every amazing women in the Safe Housing Network- all of you are #1 in my book.

Honoring these extraordinary women—justice-impacted founders and CEOs—who have built powerful organizations and are doing transformative work across the world.

- #FreeMichellewest Movement- Michelle West, and Miquelle West

- Fox Richardson-(Rob) TIME MOVIE

- Nkechi Taifa- Justice Roundtable

- Cando Clemency- Amy Povah

- Ladies of Hope Ministries-Topeka K. Sam

- Connected Kids-Rodnisha Sade Cannon

- Erika's Closet- Traletta Banks

- Operation Restoration-Syrita Steib

- RestoreHER, USA- Pamela Winn

- *Talk to Me- Foundation- Nicole Coco Davis*

- A Woman's Worth Project - Nerika "Chocolate" Jenkins

- My Meta Reentry Services, Inc- Dee Rainer

- Free Hearts -Dawn Harrington

- A little Piece of light- Donna Hylton

- Block Builderz- D'Marria Monday
- Why Not Prosper- Rev. Michelle Simmons
- Ardella's House- Toni Willis
- Silent Cry ,Inc- Shawanna Vaughn

- F.E.L.O.N- Formerly Incarcerated Empowered Leaders overcoming negative Stigmas.- Ruby Annette Carter Welch

- Forward Justice, Second Chance Federation, Daryl Atkinson, Caitlin Swain - Krisite Puckett, and all of the amazing Staff-

- *Local Support- To Sheriff Garry L. McFadden and his wife Cathy, staff- Shelby, Dorian, Georgia and Sarah and members of his team who encouraged me — thank you.*

- *To all Beauty After the Bars partners community organizations like SAVE, FICPM, Block Love, Erika's Closet, RREPS, Educate2Engage, Project Bolt, ATV, SAVE our Children's Movement, Little Listeners, Action NC, She Built this City, and so many others — your love for our people is undeniable. I am happy to fight for community with you.*

- *To the homegrown and hometown heroes from Charlotte who spoke up for me, opened doors, and refused to let my name be dragged without truth — I see you, and I honor you.*

- The Struggle, Inc. (Alesha Brown) — you are my forever sister, truly one of a kind. I love you and your incredible staff.

- Freedom Fighting Missionaries (Kenny Robinson) — you showed me what the real deal looks like: loyal, steadfast, and always having my back.

- Project BOLT (Gemini Boyd) — standing unapologetically in your truth, you continue to show your love for me and for our community.

- Kemba Pradia-Smith -Thank you for working hard and using your personal story to change policy & to bring aware awareness to systems of injustices.

Your movie KEMBA is very much needed, powerful & inspiring.

There are so many of you that — your work changed my life and the lives of so many women like me.

To every grassroots leader, organizer, and advocate named or unnamed who stood with me in public and private — I am honored to stand beside you.

To Women Behind the Walls & Jailhouse Lawyers

To every woman in federal and state prisons, county jails, holding facilities, and every woman rebuilding after incarceration — this book is for you.

You are more than a number and more than a case file. Your survival is an act of resistance. Your dreams, prayers, and perseverance matter. I stand in full solidarity with you.

To the **Jailhouse Lawyers** — the thinkers, fighters, and advocates behind the walls — thank you. You turned law libraries into war rooms for justice. You changed lives from the inside out. Your brilliance is part of this movement.

To My Critics

To every person who misused my name or spoke my story without understanding it — I thank you. You became part of the refining fire that shaped me.

I forgive you — not because I have forgotten, but because I refuse to carry bitterness where God is building blessings. This season is not about revenge. It is about redemption. As I rise, I pray you find healing too.

To My Online Community

To everyone who follows me on social media, sent a message, dropped a prayer, or simply said, "Keep going" — you are part of this story. On days when the weight was heavy, your words were oxygen.

You reminded me that my voice still matters and that I am never walking alone. You are the heartbeat behind Unbreakable.

To My Partner & Personal Support

To **Roderick Graham** — thank you for loving me through the highs and the lows, for embracing me and my family with patience, faith, and grace. Your steady presence has been a quiet shelter in loud seasons.

To Jeshawn Graham — having you as my son has been a true gift from God. Thank you for your love and unwavering support.

To My Brother Cedric Dean- and your Mama Betty Dean Baker- you have proven that family does not have to share the same blood- I love you both and thank God for you. We are a real family- always will be.

Amy Parker-when they say God sends angels, I know it's true, because God sent you. Forever in my heart.

Rita Gray — you are the friend who stood with me through the storm and the fire, never leaving my side.

Marcus Massey — thank you for reminding me who we are, where we come from, and everything we are capable of becoming.

Anthony Rouse — thank you for being a father to our two daughters, and for being a true friend.

My Attorneys, Rob Heroy and Mike Greene — thank you for giving me the space to say whatever I needed to say to survive this storm. You both are simply the best.

Judge and Attorney Kimberly Best, and Attorney Habekah Cannon — thank you for your support at the very start of this storm.

Vena Vaughn- You are the humble, quiet storm—the steady source of strength behind Beauty After the Bars and every one of our success stories. Thank you for being the backbone of this work and the heart that keeps it moving forward.

Kristie Puckett- It has been a true joy working alongside you. Thank you for every time you stood with me and for me. Your sisterhood means more than I can ever put into words.

#FreeMichelleWest — fighting for your freedom from two life sentences plus fifty years. What we built when you were behind those walls- became more than survival; it became sisterhood. Thank you for being my strength and my secret weapon, even while fighting for your own freedom. We are family—now and forever.

Patrick Edwards — thank you for standing shoulder to shoulder with me, for every call and late-night text as we fought to make things happen for our sister. Your love, commitment, and support mean more to me than words can express.

Jimmie C. Gardner-It has been a true honor to know you, and to be guided in this work by your authentic love and unwavering support.

CJ & Sam- you are brothers who know what it means to fight for freedom, inside and out. Thank you for your unwavering love, strength, and support.

To my amazing people — thank you for your unwavering love, loyalty, and belief in me. During the 2025 election—and in the middle of the fire—I owe a special debt of gratitude to every donor, supporter, and rider who stood with me when it mattered most:

Even though the outcome was not what we hoped for, you stood with me in the heat, the pressure, and the fire. You showed me that this journey has never been about a title, but about purpose, courage, and community. Your support carried me, strengthened me, and will forever be part of my story. Thank you for riding with me — always.

To my justice-impacted sisters who currently hold office, who have previously served, and who have had the courage to run for office across this country — you are living proof that redemption and representation can not only coexist, but thrive. Our democracy needs your voice. Your courage, leadership, and lived experience are reshaping what power looks like and who it belongs to. Especially: Bethany Hallam, Brittanie Bogard, Cherie Cruz, Keturah Herron, LaTonya Tate, Tarra Simmons. Thank you.

Mayor Pro Tem Anderson— Southside for life. Our foundations matter, and so does serving the people with integrity and heart.

To my amazing colleagues—Councilmembers Johnson, Dr. Watlington, Ajmera and Molina— it has been an honor to serve alongside you. Your leadership, strength, and grace inspire me, and yes… Black women do rock!

Councilmember Mitchell— thank you for seeing me, accepting me as I am, and always showing respect and grace.

To City Hall CMPD and the Security Team- thank you for your service- special shout out to Officer Vikki Coston.

To those of you who may not see your name listed: please know that your love and support during one of the hardest seasons of my life mean more than words could ever express. You are forever in my heart. If any name was missed, it was not from a lack of gratitude, but simply a slip of the mind—never of the heart.

If you gave a dollar, cast a vote, sent a text, or whispered a prayer on my behalf, please know this: I felt it. And I am grateful.

In moments when everything was shaking, you reminded me that I was not standing alone.

To My Editor & Publishing Team

To **Dr. Marita Kinney** and the **Pure Thoughts Publishing team** — thank you for treating this story with sacred care. You didn't just edit my words; you honored my truth.

Your professionalism, patience, and commitment to excellence helped transform lived experience into a book that is both craft and testimony. Because of you, *Unbreakable* is more than a message — it is a movement in print.

With deep gratitude and love,
— **Dr. Tiawana Brown**

THE RISE

...

INTRODUCTION

Why I'm Writing This Now

The FBI knocked on my door in January 2025. I will never forget that day.

My neighbor texted me first, told me two people were standing at my door, a woman and a tall man. Later, I found out it was actually two women, one of them was just so tall and broad we couldn't tell from the Ring camera whether she was a woman or a man. Thank God for my good neighbors, they're always right on time.

I texted back, thanked her, and sat there trying to process what she'd just said.

By the time her message came through, the agents had already been there for a while. Mama was on the couch, peaceful as ever, retired now from Novant Health, watching her usual lineup, Andy Griffith, cowboys and Indians, her comfort zone. She called upstairs, her voice steady and unbothered:

"Tiawana, two people are at the door."

I yelled back from the bathroom, "Mama, I'm in the bath, answer the door!"

She said, "I'm not answering nothing. They can wait on you."

So I did what only a woman like me would do, I answered the door from my bath. (using the ring camera Audio)

"Hello," I said. "How can I help you?"

One of them replied, "We're looking for Tiawana Brown."

I corrected them gently, "That would be Councilmember Tiawana Brown."

They nodded. "Yes, ma'am."

"Who are you," I asked, "and how can I help you?"

"We're with the FBI," one of them said calmly.

I took a breath.
"Okay. Give me a few minutes, I'll be right down."

Truthfully, I had no idea what the FBI wanted and why they were at my doorsteps- Never in my mind did I imagine they were standing at my door for me.

I never imagined that after thirty-five years of redemption, rebuilding, and reclaiming my life, I would face another storm, public, painful, and personal.

On May 22, 2025, it was publicly announced that I was indicted alongside my daughters on allegations that shook the city and tested every ounce of strength I have built. The headlines were loud, the judgment swift, and the whispers endless.

I watched as people who once cheered for my victory began questioning my integrity, not because they knew the truth, but because the world loves a scandal more than a testimony.

I could have hidden.
I could have let shame swallow me whole.
But that's not who I am anymore.

See, I have already lived through the kind of pain that tries to bury you. I have already been the woman people counted out, talked about, and locked away.
I have already rebuilt my life from ashes once, and this time, I know how to rise faster, stronger, and with even more faith.

This time, I'm not running from the fire.

I am standing in it, because I know who I am, and I know who God is.

I am writing this now because I want people to understand something:

Redemption doesn't expire.

It doesn't lose its power when life gets hard again.
It doesn't disappear just because people stop believing in you.
Redemption is a daily walk, a lifelong process, and I am still walking it, boldly, publicly, unapologetically.

I am also writing this because my story isn't just my own.
It belongs to every person who has fallen and gotten back up.

To every mother who has cried through the night trying to protect her children.
To every justice-impacted person who has had to prove their worth twice over just to be seen as human.

This is for the ones who know what it's like to be misunderstood and misrepresented, and still show up anyway.

I am not writing to convince anyone of my innocence. I am writing to show what it means to survive storms with dignity, to keep your head high even when the world tries to break you. To remind people that faith doesn't promise an easy life, it promises the strength to endure a hard one.

I am still standing because grace stood with me.

And if you are reading this, I want you to know this:

Whatever they have said about you,
Whatever you have survived,
Whatever storms you have had to face,

You can come back from anything.
You can walk through the fire and still smell like freedom.

This isn't my downfall.
This is just another chapter in a story that God is still writing.

When the door closed that day, something in me opened. I knew the road ahead would test every lesson I had ever learned about faith, forgiveness, and fortitude. But I also knew this, God didn't bring me this far to abandon me in the middle of the storm. I had walked through fire before, and this time, I was ready to face it with open eyes, a steady heart, and the full weight of my truth.

I walked away from that door and had to face the hardest part, telling my mama that the FBI had been there for me. Her daughter. The City Councilwoman who made it from the hood to City Hall. The People's Champ. She stood by the kitchen sink, her shoulders slumped, tears gathering in her eyes, disbelief written all over her face. After a long pause, she said quietly, "You'll have to call your sister and your aunt. I'm not telling anyone."

That moment broke something and built something all at once. It reminded me that even when the world grows loud, family feels every echo. And before I tell you what happened next, you need to understand the women who raised me, the foundation that made me unbreakable.

I need you to understand where I came from, the roots, the lessons, and the women who shaped the fighter in me.

— **Dr. Tiawana Brown**
Charlotte City Council, District 3
The People's Champion • Still Standing. Still Serving. Still Unbreakable.

INTERLUDE

The Women Who Raised Me

Before I ever learned how to fight in public, I learned how to stand tall in the kitchen, the living room, and the pew. The women who raised me were not perfect, but they were powerful. They were the kind of women who could turn struggle into survival and silence into strength.

My great-grandmother, Artie, was short in stature but mighty in spirit. She was the matriarch whose name carried through generations. My mama was named after her, a living reminder of her strength and grace. My Aunt Elizabeth, Aunt Liz, and my Grandma Artie shared that same power and poise. When I was younger, I loved visiting them in Norristown, Pennsylvania, not far from Philadelphia. Those trips felt like stepping into another world. We would go shopping at King of Prussia Mall, one of the biggest malls I had ever seen, and Aunt Liz would glide through the stores like royalty.

Her home was a masterpiece, three floors high, with furniture that looked like it belonged in a magazine. Every corner gleamed with pride and elegance. Aunt Liz drove a luxury car, dressed like she had a personal stylist, and carried herself like a woman who knew exactly who she was. Visiting her felt like being in a movie. The cousins from up north, the basketball courts filled with some fine guys, it was the 90s, reminded me of the Ruckers Tournaments in NYC, I was young, wide-eyed, and soaking up every moment. The smell of good food, the laughter, and the corner stores that sold everything from penny candy to dreams made those visits unforgettable.

And when we ventured into downtown Philadelphia, it was like entering a universe that pulsed with color, rhythm, and life. South Street was magic. The crowds, the music, the fashion, the energy, it all felt electric. There was nothing like that in downtown Charlotte. For a little girl from the Carolinas, Philly was pure wonder.

Aunt Liz knew everybody. She was the who's who of Norristown, and everything she did was wrapped in prayer. I will never forget the time one of my cousins asked to see my gold jewelry. I told her, plain as day, "I don't take my jewelry off." Aunt Liz looked at me, smiled, and said, "I like your style." That moment meant everything. It felt like getting the royal seal of approval.

Then there was my Grandma Lula, Aunt Liz's sister, aka my grandma - a praying woman through and through. Calm, strong, and steady. She did not curse, but if she ever did, you knew you were in trouble. Grandma's house on Cowles Road in Historic Revolution Park is still standing today, a true safe haven. That house saw everything, from discipline to laughter to unconditional love.

We got on the school bus there and got off there too. Grandma would walk us to the bus stop in the morning and meet us there in the afternoon. We stayed with her when our parents worked, when we got in trouble, and whenever we needed a little extra love. She would send us outside to pick our own switches when we acted up, but her love and prayers never wavered. On Sundays, she went to church dressed sharp, hat and all, until she physically could not anymore.

And then there is my mama, my foundation, my heartbeat, named after my great-grandmother Artie. Mama started working at fourteen and did not stop until she retired at sixty-five. That is more than fifty years of hard work and faithfulness. I got my work ethic straight from her. She made some of her own clothes, supported her mother constantly, and still managed to show up looking like a runway model. Mama was beautiful, a real fox, the kind of woman who turned heads and softened hearts at the same time. She worked hard, prayed harder, and raised us to do both.

I also had four aunts, each remarkable in her own way. Aunt Valerie was the smart one, educated, stylish, and full of grace. She taught aerobics, modeled, and reminded us that education was power. She kept her finances in order and her priorities straight. Later, she became a deacon in our church, proof that beauty and brains can walk hand in hand with faith.

Aunt Shirley was the caregiver for all of us, and for our children, and some of our children's children. She was the family beautician, washing our hair in the bathtub or sometimes the kitchen sink. She would lather us up with conditioner, part our hair with surgeon level precision, and rub in that royal blue hair grease like it was holy oil. Then came the blow dryer and the straightening comb. You always knew the sizzle was coming when the grease hit that hot metal. It was not intentional when she burned us a little, but it was part of the ritual. And somehow, the finished product was always beautiful, with long pigtails tied up in bright bows for Sunday service.

Aunt Linda became one of my favorites. I loved visiting her and talking for hours. She had a calm and listening spirit, and she made the best potato salad this side of heaven. Aunt Linda would be so proud of me today. I know that for certain.

Then there was Aunt Deborah, the baby sister, sweet as sweet potato pie. Always smiling, always asking questions, sometimes the same ones over and over. She reminded me constantly that the best things in life are free. Her joy was contagious. She, Aunt Linda, and Grandma Lula Mae are all in heaven now, but their presence is still felt.

And I cannot forget my cousin, Barbara Phillips. She was raised right alongside my mama and my aunts, and her voice was a gift straight from heaven. She sang at every family function and made sure no one left empty-handed. Barbara believed in generosity. She lived it. She was the embodiment of God's love.

As we sat around listening to stories about Southside Homes and Brookhill, people often said my mama was a fighter, that she took care of business and did not play. I learned that firsthand when I was little. She found out a school bully had been picking on me, and that was the end of it. She met me in the park at the center of Southside Homes, right by the sliding board, and waited for that bully to show up. Mama did not just protect me, she made sure I learned to protect myself. The first time I came home crying was the last time.

These women, my great-grandma Artie, my grandmothers, my mama, my aunts, and my cousins, were the architects of my spirit. They taught me resilience through prayer, confidence through presence, and elegance through example. They showed me that faith is not a Sunday act, but a daily walk, and that love is something you do, not just something you say.

Before I ever had a title or a spotlight, I had them. And every time I rise, I rise with their names written in my spirit.

That day in the park was my first real lesson in standing up for myself. It was also the day I realized exactly where my fight came from. It came from her, my mama, and from every woman before her who refused to bow to fear. Southside and Brookhill were not just places on a map. They were classrooms where we learned toughness, loyalty, and love the hard way. The playgrounds, the porches, and the laughter echoing through those brick walls shaped me long before any title ever did.

Before the city lights, before the microphones, before the nameplate on the dais, there was Southside Homes. And that is where the story truly began.

CHAPTER 1

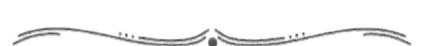

Southside Housing Project: Humble Beginnings

Before I ever dreamed of City Hall, I was just a little girl running through the red clay of Southside Homes, barefoot sometimes, bold most of the time, and loved by a village that did not have much but always had enough. Southside was more than a housing project. It was a world of its own, the kind of place where everybody knew everybody, where kids played outside until the streetlights came on, and where mamas called your name loud enough for the whole block to hear.

The air carried the smell of frying chicken, hair grease, and summer heat. You could hear laughter mixed with music, the sound of Frankie Beverly and Maze floating through open windows, or gospel on Sunday mornings. Southside was tough, but it had heart, the kind of heart that made you strong long before you knew what strength meant.

Our neighbors were like family. If one child got in trouble, the whole block knew before the sun went down. If someone was hungry, a plate would show up at your door, no questions asked. It was a place where people survived together, not alone.

My mama's reputation stretched across those streets like protection. Everyone knew Miss Brown did not play about her only two daughters. She was firm, fair, and fierce, the kind of mother whose love came with rules, prayers, and that one look that could stop you mid-sentence. But behind her strength was softness. She laughed often, cooked big, and kept our home full of light even when life got dark.

Looking back now, I realize Southside Homes was the training ground for everything I would become. The fighter, the advocate, the survivor. The lessons I learned there did not come from books. They came from front porches, church pews, and the women who taught me that dignity and determination could grow anywhere, even in the projects.

The Foundation That Built Me

Southside Homes in Charlotte, North Carolina, once part of the Charlotte Housing Authority and now known as Inlivian, was where my story began. Many saw it as "just another set of projects." For me, it was the foundation of everything I would one day become.

I was surrounded by love, shaped by a long line of phenomenal Black women who carried strength in their bones and faith in their hearts. They were my first teachers, my guardians, and my compass.

My mother, Artie Mae Brown, stood tall through every storm.
My grandparents, Lula M. Brown and J. W. Brown, now watch over me from Heaven. They were the backbone of our family, hardworking and devoted.

My aunts, Valarie Brown Gardner, Shirley Brown, and Barbara Phillips, along with my angels in Heaven, Alinda Brown and Deborah Brown, each reflected God's grace in their own way.

My uncle, Jerry "Redhead" Brown, who now rests with them, taught me that family is not perfect but love is powerful.

My sister, Chunta Olaseha, remains my confidant, my steady place, and the reminder that blood runs deeper than pain.

My cousins, Barbara, Monique, Monica, and Antavia, each wrote their own chapter of resilience in our shared story.

And then there are my daughters, Antoinette and Tijema, the greatest lessons I ever learned about unconditional love.

My first and only grandson, Byron B. Sadler Jr., is the heartbeat of our next generation, proof that legacy is alive.

I grew up learning and in programs at the Historic Bethlehem Center, a place that no longer stands but shaped the community I carried with me. It was there I learned discipline, responsibility, and the quiet dignity of service.

My Mama's Walk

My mother was one of the hardest-working women I have ever known. She did not simply raise a family. She walked her way through survival.

Every morning she left Southside Homes and headed down Remount Road, her stride steady, her purpose fixed. WGIV Radio Station stood proudly along that stretch, the heartbeat of the community. As she crossed the bridge, the hum of traffic from I-77 rose beneath her feet, a sound etched forever in my memory.

She was in restaurant management at Kentucky Fried Chicken at 1600 Remount Road on the corner of West Boulevard and Remount. Today it is Nick's Restaurant; before that, it was a Jack in the Box. Across the street stood The Grapevine, a Black-owned convenience store where neighbors swapped stories and kids bought penny candy.

Behind KFC was Wayne's Supermarket, a small grocery store built on trust. You could get a loaf of bread, a pack of meat, maybe a gallon of Jungle Juice, and pay your tab at the end of the week. No contracts. No judgment. Just community.

That kind of neighborhood credit barely exists today, but back then, it was how we survived between paychecks.

I walked that same Remount Road bridge many days with my Uncle Red, my protector in every sense of the word. He was loved everywhere he went—Southside, Brookhill, South Tryon, Bank Street, Chicago Avenue. His name carried weight. The gentrification of today has changed those streets, but back then, they were full of life.

That bridge connected everything that made up my world, from PAL cheerleading practice to football games to summers at Revolution Park Swimming Pool, where we learned to swim and dream. It led to Grandma Lula's house on Cowles Road, which still stands today, and to Mama's job, where faith, food, and service met.

I cannot count how many people I took to Mama's job to eat. Friends, neighbors, kids who were hungry. Mama fed the West Boulevard and Remount Road community one plate at a time. That KFC kitchen was her ministry long before I ever had a title of my own.

At home, it was me and my little sister. Mama worked long hours, sometimes double shifts, so we spent a lot of time alone. Even when money was tight, Mama made sure we were dressed to impress. Matching outfits, polished shoes, pressed hair. We were the cream of the crop in the projects, walking proof that pride does not depend on money.

Yes, there were times I got into things Mama would have torn me up for if she had known. Little adventures, childish curiosity, moments of mischief that still make me smile. But even then, I was learning. I was learning independence, what it meant to grow up fast, to watch the door close behind Mama and feel both freedom and responsibility rise in my chest.

My mother's steps down that road taught me that strength does not always roar. Sometimes it whispers through worn shoes and tired feet, saying keep going anyway. Mama had her faith and her determination, and she walked it out each day.

She was a fox and she knew it. She looked like a model, like she had stepped straight out of Jet Magazine's Beauty of the Week. Pretty as ever and full of grace.

And yes, I get it from my mama.

Life in Southside Homes

Life in Southside Homes moved to its own rhythm. Mornings smelled like biscuits and bacon from one apartment and hair grease from another. Radios blasted gospel or WGIV, and children's voices echoed across the courtyards before the sun climbed too high. It was not fancy, but it was home.

Once Mama left, the neighborhood came alive. Kids poured out from every direction. Jump ropes snapped against the pavement. Boys dribbled basketballs. Girls double-dutched. Our drill team marched up and down the street while the neighborhood watched. Clapping hands, childhood rhymes, laughter rising like music. We did not have much, but we made joy out of everything. A busted bike could become a race car. An old milk crate was enough for a basketball hoop.

We played games that required nothing but imagination, Box of Color, Tweet Little Leet, hide-and-seek, and every childhood game that kept our spirits light.

In Southside, people looked out for one another. Miss Johnson across the way would call out from her porch if she saw anything that didn't look right. Mr. Jackson, much like my Uncle Red, was the unofficial handyman, fixing anything with duct tape, a hammer, and a prayer. And on Fridays, when paychecks came in, the whole block felt lighter. Laughter grew louder, music got stronger, and the air smelled like fried fish and hope.

The Historic Bethlehem Center was both strict and sacred. It taught us community, responsibility, and worth. The teachers there demanded excellence because they knew the world would not give us any passes. Miss Rose and Miss Blondie, our dance teachers, truly were the best. Friday night discos and Teen Time with Mr. King felt like magic. I snuck in more times than I should have, always getting in trouble for being underage, but loving every minute.

Revolution Park was one of my favorite places. The pool shimmered under the Carolina sun, and kids from Southside and Brookhill, Revolution Park, Clanton Park, and all areas of West Blvd came together. We jumped off the edge, splashed each other, and sat on the concrete talking about who liked who. Revolution Park was freedom, a place where kids like us could dream beyond our circumstances.

No matter how far we roamed, we always made our way home before the streetlights flickered on. You did not want your mama calling your full name out that window. That meant business.

Southside was love—real, raw, unfiltered love. It was where I learned to laugh through tears, to keep my head high even when we had little, and to fight for what mattered. It was where I discovered that being "from the projects" did not define my worth. It prepared me for the fire I would face later in life.

Those red-clay streets taught me pride, grit, and grace. And long before I became Councilmember Brown, I was just Tiawana, a little girl from Southside, dreaming bigger than her circumstances and holding tight to the lessons my mama taught me: stand tall, work hard, pray daily, and never let anyone make you feel small.

CHAPTER 2

The Streets, the Cheerleader, and the First Hit

I was sixteen, popular, a cheerleader, and caught up in a world I did not fully understand. I was drawn to the street guys, men who moved fast, spent money freely, and carried danger in their eyes. One of them stole my heart. He was handsome, charming, and from Miami, smooth-talking and dangerous all at once.

Mama knew I had a boyfriend, but she did not know the truth, that he had already started hitting me. My little sister saw it first. She saw him hit me in my face with a full fist , and that was the day everything changed. My protector, the sister I had always shielded, became my defender. She ran to my mama and told her everything- not before she challenged my abuser- if you hit my sister again- it will be your last! My sister meant every word!

Mama did not waste a second. She showed up, fiery, fearless, and straight from the heart of Southside. I still remember standing beside her when she confronted him.

"Keep your damn hands off my child, you hear me? I am not one of them women you play with. Leave her alone and keep your hands off her."

Her voice did not shake. Her hands did not tremble. She pointed at him, then at me, and in that moment, I saw what strength looked like in human form.

But even that did not stop the cycle.

He was an abuser, and the truth is, the abuse did not stop. Even after Mama's warning, even after the neighbors whispered, he found his way back into my life. That is what abusers do, they come back with promises and tears, and when you are young and still learning what love really is, you want to believe them.

He had other women. I caught him more than once, the lies, the cheating, the phone calls that did not make sense. He was doing everything street guys did, living fast and reckless, and somehow, I kept getting pulled back into his world.

I thought I could fix him. I thought if I loved him enough, prayed enough, or stayed loyal enough, he would change. But instead, the pain just changed shape.

Then I found out I was pregnant. I was in college, young, scared, and trying to figure out how to be a mother when I was still growing up myself. I was carrying my first child, my beautiful Antoinette, and I remember praying every night,

"Lord, please save me. Please save my baby. Please get me out."

And God answered, not the way I expected, but the way I needed. He was arrested and went to jail.

I will never forget the mix of emotions, the relief, the guilt, the quiet peace that finally came after years of noise and fear. I did not want him in jail, but I knew that was the only way I could breathe again.

It was 1992. I was a student at Livingstone College, trying to balance classes, pregnancy, and the emotional wreckage that abuse leaves behind. I knew I had to make a change, so I transferred to Johnson C. Smith University. That move, from one campus to another, from chaos to clarity, became the start of my next chapter.

I was still young, still learning, still praying, but something in me was shifting. I was beginning to understand that survival was not enough. I wanted to live.

I did not want to leave Livingstone College. That campus had become my home, my safe place, my joy, my escape. I had good friends there, real ones, cheerleaders, athletes, professors, and classmates who saw me as more than what I was going through. Some of those same people are still in my life today. We still talk, still check in, still share memories from a time when life felt simpler.

But back then, I was an emotional mess. Antoinette's daddy was in prison, and I was just trying to hold myself together. I had no idea that I was on my own path to prison too. That was not supposed to be my story. I was supposed to graduate, make my mama proud, and build a better life for my baby.

My mindset was survival mode, one foot in front of the other. I just needed to get home. Home to my village. To my mama, Aunt Nesie, Grandma Lula, Aunt Shirley, and my little sister, the same one I had left behind with Mama when I first went off to school. I needed them now more than ever.

Transferring to Johnson C. Smith University felt like the right move. It meant I could be closer to Antoinette, to my family, to my support system. It meant I could keep going to school while knowing my baby girl was being loved and cared for by the same people who had loved me through everything.

Back home, I had help, a real village that stepped in without judgment. My baby was surrounded by love, and that gave me the strength to keep showing up to class, even when my heart was heavy.

What I did not know was that this move, meant to bring stability, would also become the beginning of another storm. It was on the campus of JCSU where the next chapter of my life began, where survival collided with circumstance, where I would soon face the mistakes that would lead me straight into the federal system.

Two years after giving birth to Antoinette, I would find myself pregnant again, this time with her sister, Tijema, and on my way to face a new reality I could have never imagined, the Federal Bureau of Prisons.

But even in that moment, young, scared, and standing between two worlds, I held on to what I knew best, faith, family, and fight. Because that is what Southside raised me to do.

I liked street guys, men with flash, confidence, and the kind of swagger that made the room stop. They had money, cars, jewelry, and influence, and at that age, I was drawn to it all. I loved the atmosphere, the energy of the night, the way we walked into a room and owned it.

I was still so young, moving at a pace where God must have looked down and said, "My daughter, I have to slow you down."

The truth is, I never drank. I never smoked. I just liked being around life, the lights, the laughter, the music. My friends and I, our clique, were one of the hottest in the city. In our minds, it was all about us.

Weekends meant Freedom Park, where the best-looking cars cruised from West Boulevard down East Boulevard. Sundays after church at Greater Mt. Sinai Baptist Church at 1243 West Boulevard, the same church that raised me and still grounds me today, I would put Antoinette in her little cloth baby carrier and take her right along with me to the park. I was a proud mother, even in my mess.

When the Freedom Park scene faded, we cruised Beattie's Ford Road, past Johnson C. Smith, Historic Excelsior Club, Friendship Baptist church and many spots to arrive at Hornets Park. Everyone wanted to be seen, the cars, the fashion, the music, it was the heartbeat of young Black Charlotte.

The nightlife was our playground, Choppa Lounge and Casanova on West Boulevard, adjacent to one another-pulsing with energy. We hit Queen's Park Movie Theatre, Skate Palace, and Kate's Skating Rink, where the best skaters in the city hit the floor and the rest of us watched in awe. My girls and I had matching skates, matching outfits, and matching confidence.

We were beautiful, bold, and fearless, and if you crossed us, we could fight too. Cute did not mean soft. We could throw those bows in the parking lot and still show up the next Sunday in church singing "Amazing Grace."

It was all part of my journey, the glitter, the grit, the growing pains. I did not see it then, but God was writing the story that would one day make me unbreakable.

CHAPTER 3

A Box Checked

When I came home from the hospital with Antoinette, I was still just a girl trying to figure out what womanhood really meant. I had traded cheerleading uniforms for diaper bags, textbooks for baby bottles, and parties for sleepless nights.

I did not wake up one morning and decide to go to prison. Nobody does.

The road that took me there was paved with good intentions, bad choices, and the kind of pain that makes you numb to warning signs. I was in my early twenties, juggling motherhood, college, and survival, still trying to figure out who I was while pretending I already knew.

After transferring to Johnson C. Smith University, life moved fast. Between classes, working part time, and raising Antoinette, I was stretched thin but determined. On the outside, I looked like I had it all together, the girl who smiled through everything. But behind that smile was exhaustion, fear, and a hunger for stability that made me vulnerable to anything that looked like help.

The truth is, I was still healing, from abuse, disappointment, and the pressure of trying to grow up too soon. In that fragile space, I started reconnecting with old friends, some good, some not. Street life was still around me. It was familiar. It did not judge. And when you are trying to hold on to your dignity while the world keeps knocking you down, familiarity can feel like comfort, even when it is dangerous.

I never planned to get involved in anything illegal. I was just trying to make it, to keep food on the table, to keep my child in daycare, to pay tuition, to keep the lights on. But the streets have a way of pulling you back in, especially when they know your name and your hustle.

One decision turned into another.
A favor became a habit.
And before I realized it, I was caught up in something bigger than I ever imagined.

I remember the day everything shifted, the moment when "helping out" stopped being harmless. The cars, the fast money, the connections, it all felt like an opportunity at first. But in reality, it was a trap disguised as a blessing.

By the time I realized the weight of what I was part of, it was too late. The feds were already watching.

I was young, smart, and naive enough to believe that if you were not the one holding the product, you could not get in trouble. But that is not how the system works, especially for young Black women caught in the web of other people's choices.

When the indictment came, it was like time stopped. My name, **Tiawana Brown,** printed in bold letters across paperwork I did not fully understand. My world shattered in an instant. The same girl who once wore a cheerleading uniform and dreamed of graduating college was now standing on the edge of a federal case.

Mama cried the first time she found out. She did not yell. She did not curse. She just sat at the kitchen table, her hands folded, her eyes full of pain and disbelief. She looked at me and said,

"Baby, this ain't you. You were raised better than this. But no matter what happens, you're still mine."

Those words broke me and healed me all at once.

I was facing time in federal prison. The reality hit hard, like a brick to the chest. I was no longer just somebody's daughter or student. I was an inmate waiting to transition into the cage.

The hardest part was not the thought of prison itself. It was leaving my daughters. Antoinette was just a toddler, and I was pregnant with Tijema. The guilt ate away at me. I had spent years trying to protect my children from pain, and now I was the one causing it.

I prayed like I had never prayed before.
I begged God for mercy, for forgiveness, for another chance.
And even though my circumstances did not change right away, something inside me did.

That is where my next chapter began, the chapter that would test my faith, reshape my identity, and rebuild my purpose from the inside out.

Because what the world saw as a downfall, God was already rewriting as my redemption.

But even with all that, I was still a cheerleader.
At Johnson C. Smith University, I alternated between my cheerleading uniform and my diaper bag, performing on the sidelines, studying in between feedings, and pushing through exhaustion.

I was young, determined, and driven by something bigger than pride.

The whispers came quickly, and the rumors followed. Some came from strangers, but some came from people I loved, friends, classmates, even family who did not understand my choices. They did not see the full picture. They only saw the surface.

But I kept pushing. I wanted my education, and I was not going to let judgment take that away from me.

I had male friends at JCSU, good people who respected me, supported me, and made me laugh when life felt heavy. I was still popular, still smiling, still showing up.

I had a new 300ZX, one of the hottest cars on campus, and I drove it like a symbol, proof that I was still standing, still shining, even when life was trying to dim my light.

But even then, I lived with caution.
I did things more quietly, more carefully. Not because I was ashamed but because I had learned how quickly love could turn into judgment.

What I did not realize at the time was that society had already started checking boxes beside my name:

Black, young, single mother.

Those boxes followed me everywhere, into classrooms, into interviews, into every space where people thought they had the right to define me before I could even introduce myself.

And later, after prison, there would be another box, the one that asked,

"Have you ever been convicted of a felony?"

That box does not just follow you, it shadows you. It becomes the test of how much you believe in your own redemption.

But back then, I did not know all that yet.
All I knew was that I loved my baby and wanted a better life for her.

I was juggling motherhood, education, and survival while the world watched to see if I would fail. The same people who once cheered for me on the sidelines now whispered when I walked by.

But what they did not know was that I came from Southside, from a long line of women who knew how to stretch faith further than money and carry the weight of the world in high heels and a smile.

So I kept going.
I went to class. I showed up for practice. I studied when I could.
And I carried Antoinette everywhere, on my hip, in my arms, and in my heart every single step of the way.

Motherhood made me stronger, but it also made me invisible to some people. Yet I refused to disappear.

Because once you have been labeled, you have two choices,
You can live under it, or you can redefine it.
I chose the latter.

Transitional Closing: From the Fall to the Fire

Looking back now, I see that every step, every mistake, every heartbreak, and every sleepless night was preparing me for the woman I would become. I did not know it then, but God was already building the bridge that would carry me from pain to purpose.

The world called it a downfall.
I call it divine redirection.

When I finally stood before that prison gate, I was not just walking into a sentence. I was walking into my refining. I was scared, yes, but I felt something deeper stirring inside me, a quiet knowing that this was not the end of my story. It was the beginning of the fire that would forge my faith, my strength, and my voice.

When I walked through those prison doors for the first time, the air felt heavy, like stepping into another world. The clanging of gates, the sound of footsteps echoing off concrete floors, the faces of women who looked just like me but carried stories of their own. Because sometimes God allows the storm not to destroy you, but to reveal who you really are.

CHAPTER 4

The Fast Life, The Fall, and The Faith

I got pregnant with my second daughter, Tijema, while I was a student at Johnson C. Smith University.
By then, the federal charges were already in motion.
I just didn't know how deep the storm would get.

I had gotten used to the fast life.
The money, the attention, the nightlife.
After years of living in survival mode, fast felt like safety.
It felt like control.

But I didn't realize that the same speed that once made me feel alive was about to take everything away.

The truth is, I got caught up.
I got mixed up with a group of people on campus who were running student loan schemes, just young people chasing easy money, taking advantage of a system that handed out funds with no checks and no balance.

I never thought it would lead me to a federal prison cage.
We were young and reckless, too confident to think about consequences, too eager to slow down.

But the system, it never forgets.
It waits. It watches. And when it comes, it comes hard, especially for people who look like us.

College students aren't exempt from the scars of the criminal legal system.
We were supposed to be preparing for careers and bright futures, and instead we were getting a firsthand education in how injustice works up close.

At that time, I was living fast and loving it.
I liked nice things, the clothes, the cars, the jewelry, the feeling of walking into a club and being seen.

I was the girl who only wanted men with money, and not just a little. If you didn't have it, you couldn't sit at my table.

Tijema's father was part of that world too, but he wasn't just anybody. He was the one.

In the streets, he was the who's who. Nothing in the city moved unless it came through him.
He had money, and lots of it.
He was charming, powerful, and dangerous in ways I didn't fully see at the time.

We weren't a couple, but we hung out, got money together, and lived in that whirlwind of late nights, loud music, and quick cash.

When I found out I was pregnant, I wasn't happy.
But the truth is, I wasn't surprised either.
I wasn't using protection.
I was too busy chasing life to think about what life was chasing me.

When I say we had it going on, I mean it, at least on the surface. We looked good. We moved fast. We thought we were untouchable.

But behind all that shine was a slow unraveling that none of us saw coming.

When I left for prison, he left for the streets, and that was the end of that chapter.

But in the middle of all that chaos, God still had His hand on me. He let me fall, but only far enough to make me reach for Him again.

That is the thing about the fast life.
It makes you feel powerful until it proves how powerless you really are.

By the time my sentence was handed down, the fast life had come to a slow, painful stop.
The lights went out, the phones went silent, and the people who once called my name disappeared one by one.

The girl who once cheered under Friday night lights was now packing government issued uniforms, trying to hold back tears in front of her family.

I was scared as heck, more scared than I had ever been in my life, because I didn't want to go to prison. I didn't want to leave my babies. I didn't want to face what waited for me on the other side of those gates.

But even in my fear, I knew one thing for certain.
I still had my mama.

My mama was my anchor.
The same woman who had stood in that park years ago to protect me was still standing for me now, praying, believing, holding me together when I was falling apart.

When the morning came to leave for Alderson, West Virginia, I stood at the edge of a new reality, scared, humbled, and surrendered. I didn't know what waited for me beyond those gates, but I knew I wasn't the same girl who chased the fast life.

I was a woman learning to face her consequences with courage, holding tight to faith, family, and my mama's strength to carry me through.

CHAPTER 5

The Ride to Alderson

The morning was cold, and my heart was even colder. It was March, and the world around me felt heavy with silence. Every mile we drove through those mountains felt like I was being pulled further and further away from everything I loved.

The air was thin, sharp, and still. Snow rested on the roofs of the old country homes we passed, their tops blanketed in white like frozen memories. The houses were few and far apart, scattered across long stretches of land and endless trees that seemed to whisper my fears right back to me.

I remember thinking, *I'm in the middle of nowhere.*

I was scared. Crying in disbelief. My heart beating fast and slow all at once.

Mama sat in the front passenger seat, her friend driving us deeper into those mountains. I sat behind the driver so Mama could see me. Every few minutes she reached her hand back to touch my leg — her silent way of saying, *I'm still here.* It was all the comfort she could give. I saw the tears forming in her eyes, even as she tried to stay strong for me.

As we got closer, reality began to suffocate me. The car grew quieter, and the snow-covered trees felt like they were closing in on us, closing in on me.

When we finally pulled into the gates of Alderson Federal Prison Camp, it hit me like a wall.

This was real.

Mama and her friend were dropping me off at a federal prison in the middle of nowhere.

There was no Antoinette, my two-year-old baby.
No comfort.
No family.
No Mama.
No little sister.
No village.

Just me — and Tijema growing inside my stomach.

Mama reached for my hand before I stepped out.
"You're going to be okay," she said softly, her voice trembling.

When I stepped out, I held her with everything in me — my nails, my tears, my heart. They had to pry us apart. That embrace was the last warmth I'd feel for a long time.

I walked toward those cold gray gates, and the moment I stepped inside, my world changed.

I was met not with compassion or understanding, but with procedure — cold, inhumane, and humiliating.

They stripped me of my clothes, my dignity, and my sense of self.

Strip.
Squat.
Cough.
Say "ahh."
Lift your feet.
Turn around.
Repeat.

It was like being examined by a doctor, except this time, there was no care in their eyes, no humanity in their tone. Every woman entering that prison, pregnant or not, went through the same ritual. There were no exceptions behind those cold federal walls.

Standing there, naked, vulnerable, and pregnant, I felt the full weight of what incarceration really meant.

You weren't just locked up.
You were broken down, piece by piece, layer by layer, until the system thought it owned your soul.

But even then, even in that moment, something deep inside me refused to break.

I whispered a prayer under my breath, one that would carry me through the years ahead:
"God, don't let them take my spirit."

The sound of the gates closing behind me was the loudest silence I'd ever heard. It echoed in my mind like a funeral bell, a reminder that life as I knew it had changed forever.

I thought of Mama's tears.
My baby's face.
My little sister — still in high school, forced to grow up too fast, stepping into shoes that weren't meant for her yet.

I was torn apart thinking of all the pain I had caused — my Mama, my little sister, my family, the people who loved me and didn't deserve the heartbreak I was bringing them.

How did I get here?
How did I become **10567-058**?

A number.
A sentence.
A memory that would mark me for life.

But even in that pain, deep in the quiet places of my spirit, there was a whisper — the same whisper that had carried me through every storm:

This is not the end.

CHAPTER 6

The First Day Inside Alderson

Mama was about to pull off when a tall, slender guard in gray pants and a crisp white shirt with a small black bow tie — the standard Bureau of Prisons uniform — walked toward the car. She didn't carry a gun. Her glasses framed kind eyes that somehow stood out against the cold backdrop of Alderson, West Virginia. Snow covered the ground in patches, and I could see women walking across the compound in heavy coats, their heads down as the cold cut through the silence.

For those who don't know, Alderson Federal Prison was established in 1927 and originally called the Federal Industrial Institution for Women. It was the first federal prison built exclusively for women, and they tried to make it look like a boarding school instead of a prison. Cottage-style housing instead of cells. A campus feel instead of concrete and steel.

It opened with 174 women. By the time I self-surrendered on that cold March day in 1994, there were hundreds.

The town of Alderson was small, quiet, and known nationwide for only one thing, the women's federal prison camp. Years later, it got the nickname "Camp Cupcake" when Martha Stewart served time there, but trust me, there was nothing sweet about that place. I don't care what they called it on TV. Prison is prison. And no matter how they try to dress it up, it was never designed for women. Hygiene, maternal care, basic necessities, everything was a struggle. Something as simple as getting sanitary napkins was a battle.

That tall guard, who I'd later learn was Mrs. Wills, walked around to my side of the car and gently said, "Come on out, sweetheart."

She was a white woman with a thick southern accent, warm but firm. I froze in place.
Mama got out first, and I instantly grabbed onto her. I cried hard and uncontrollably, as if holding her tighter could somehow force the moment to stop. But eventually, they had to pry us apart.

Mama was gone.
And I was alone.

My first day inside wasn't like the stories people tell on TV. It was worse. The intake process was cold, inhumane, and humiliating.

The inhumane conditions- replayed and repeated....

All I could think about was-They told me to squat and cough.
To spread my buttocks.
To lift each foot.
To open my mouth and say "ahh."

There I was, six and a half months pregnant, standing in a medical room inside R&D —Receiving and Discharge, trying to hold myself together while they stripped me of every piece of dignity I had left.

When it was over, all I could think was, *Why can't I stay home and have my baby?*

I rubbed my belly, whispering to my unborn daughter, making sure she was still okay.

They placed me in a temporary dorm with other women who were just arriving, all of us waiting to be processed and assigned to our cottages. Someone mentioned there was a special unit for pregnant women, and I prayed I'd be moved there soon.

Life inside Alderson moved in rhythms.

Long lines for the phone, fifteen-minute calls, you had to have money on your books/commissary to make a call.

Cold, bland food in the chow hall.

The 4:00 p.m. count, when the entire Bureau of Prisons froze and every inmate had to stand still.

"Inmate Brown, 10567-058."

That was me.

My name replaced by a number.

You could always hear the guards before you saw them. Keys jingling. Boots echoing down the hallway.

Then came the mail call, the most anticipated part of the day. Every woman, no matter her background, became a child waiting for her name to be called. A letter meant hope. A letter meant somebody still remembered you.

Phone calls cost money. If I remember right, it was about $3.50 for fifteen minutes to reach my loved one in Charlotte, NC. That added up fast. You needed money on your account, and that meant waiting for someone, family, friends, anybody, to send you something. There was a limit on how many calls you could make and how much commissary you could buy.

Half the time, the items you really needed were out of stock, and the prices were high. Still, I remember the excitement of getting the commissary list, checking off things like soap, toothpaste, snacks. It wasn't much, but those little check marks gave us a small sense of control in a world where everything else was controlled for us.

By the end of my first week, I knew this was going to be a long journey.

Then came the attack.

It was about six weeks in. I was walking toward the commissary, adjusting my Walkman, a small cassette player with wired headphones, when I heard voices behind me.

"There she go, that bitch."

I didn't think they were talking about me. But before I could turn around, I was jumped.
Three women.
The first kick landed straight in my stomach.

I tried to fight back. I'm from the streets; folding was never my style. But the pain was blinding. My knees buckled. I hit the ground holding my belly as chaos exploded around me.

Guards came running. Medics rushed in. I remember a man asking, "Who did this to you?"

I said nothing.
Not one name.
Revenge would come later, I thought.

Word traveled fast in prison. The attackers were caught and taken to ADU, Administrative Detention Unit, what we called the hole.

Meanwhile, I was in the hospital for nearly two weeks fighting to keep my baby safe. My contractions wouldn't stop. I prayed day and night that God would spare her.

When things finally stabilized, the doctors made a decision.
They would induce labor on June 9, 1994.

That was the day my daughter, **Tijema**, was born.

Born inside a federal prison.
Born in the middle of a storm I had created.
Born into my fight to survive, rise, and redeem my life. Born with me in handcuffs and Shackles.

CHAPTER 7

The Birth Inside the Walls

The night before they were scheduled to drive me to the hospital to be induced, I spent every dime I had calling my mother. I clutched the receiver like it was the only thing connecting me to home. Her voice was the only thing that calmed me in that place, the only warmth I could feel through those cold federal walls.

My counselor, Mrs. Wills, the same woman who met me at the gate on my first day, told me I would be allowed to stay with my newborn for a short time after delivery. What she didn't know was that my heart was torn in two. My mother and family were preparing to come pick up the baby, but quietly, I had made another plan.

For full transparency, I hadn't planned to keep my baby.

At the time, my mind was in full survival mode. I was six and a half months pregnant, locked inside a federal prison, with a two-year-old daughter, Antoinette, waiting for me back home. My mother was already raising my little sister and had taken on more than anyone should ever have to. The thought of sending home another mouth to feed, more diapers, more milk, more sleepless nights, broke me.

I couldn't bear it.

So I made a choice that still haunts me. I arranged for my baby to be adopted. I had even chosen the parents. I convinced myself it was responsible, even noble. But deep down, the truth was simple: I was scared. Scared of raising another child from behind bars. Scared of burdening my mama even more. Scared of failing again.

Then came the voice that changed everything, my grandfather.

He didn't sugarcoat anything. He said, "If you leave that baby in the mountains, stay in prison and don't come home."

His words cut through every layer of fear I had. And just like that, the adoption ended. The couple I had chosen left the hospital empty-handed, and my daughter, my beautiful, powerful daughter, stayed in the world I almost let her slip away from.

Her name, **Tijema**, came from one of the women I met at Alderson. She told me it meant Queen, Beauty, and Power, Royalty. The moment I heard it, I knew it belonged to her. She was all of that.

When the day finally came, I went into labor and spent fourteen long hours giving birth alone. No family. No comfort. No familiar face. Just one staff member from the prison sitting in the corner.

My wrists were cuffed. My ankles were shackled.
That is no way to bring life into the world.

When they placed her on my chest, I rubbed her tiny feet and felt the soft curls on her head. She had mocha skin that glowed under the hospital lights. I counted her fingers and her toes, ten and ten. Perfect.

She was perfect.

But my pregnancy had been far from it. I had been kicked in the stomach during my last trimester. I had spent weeks in a hospital bed praying she would survive. And now, after all of that, I was being forced to leave her behind.

After just forty-eight hours, they shackled me again and walked me out of that hospital room. My body was weak. My heart was shattered. But I knew my girl would be safe because once again, my mama came through.

She drove through the mountains to West Virginia with my grandma Lula, my cousin Peewee, and others from the village. They brought my daughter home, seven pounds of pure grace.

I can still see Mama's arms wrapped around her as they told me over the phone that she was safe. Only then could I breathe.

Back at Alderson, I was a wreck. I bugged Mrs. Wills constantly, asking to call the hospital, asking if my baby was okay, asking if she was breathing, eating, being held. My anxiety was a storm. My heart bounced between guilt and gratitude, guilt for almost giving her away and gratitude that she was safe with the people who loved me most.

Even behind prison walls, with chains still on my feet, I knew one thing for certain: love had broken through.

This journey was a marathon, not a sprint.

After serving 33 and a half months, I finally came home, but not to the freedom people imagine. Freedom after incarceration is its own kind of struggle. The lack of resources waiting for me on the outside pushed me right back toward the same traps I had just escaped. Months after my release, recidivism swallowed me whole and I returned to prison.

I remember "checking the box," the words that follow you for the rest of your life:

Have you ever been convicted of a felony?

Those words shut doors before I even had a chance to knock. In the 1990s, being justice-impacted meant carrying a permanent scarlet letter.

There weren't many organizations fighting for second chances back then, but I give full credit to Goodwill, to **Verona Hendrix, Sheila Causiestko**, and **Mr. Moore** with Vocational Rehabilitation Services. They did everything they could to keep me from walking back through that revolving door. They believed in me when the system didn't.

But the system was what it was.
And depending on who you ask, it still is.

CHAPTER 8

The Healing Begins

Coming home after prison wasn't freedom. It was another kind of sentence.

The world had moved on, but it hadn't moved forward for women like me. I came home determined to make it, but everything was designed for me to fail. Employers turned me away. Apartments denied me. "Check the box" became a new set of shackles that followed me everywhere I went.

And just like that, I was back inside.

Recidivism wasn't a theory. It was my reality.
I was fighting like hell against a system that defeated me before I even had a chance to stand up. The revolving door spun fast, and walking back into those walls broke my heart. But this time, something inside me was different.

The fire that once burned with shame now burned with purpose.

I started paying attention, not just to my story, but to the women around me.

Mothers. Survivors. Fighters.

Women who looked just like me, women who were being recycled through a system that claimed to "correct" us but never prepared us to come home.

That's when I learned what recidivism really meant.
It wasn't about personal failure.
It was about lack of access.

We weren't failing society.
Society was failing us.

The Reality for Women Behind Bars

The numbers tell a truth this country still refuses to face:

- The United States incarcerates more women than any other country in the world.

- Since 1980, the number of women in prison has increased by more than **475%** (The Sentencing Project).

- Today, there are over **200,000 women** behind bars in the U.S., and **60% are mothers** of minor children.

- Nearly **80%** of incarcerated women are survivors of sexual abuse, violence, or trauma.

- And Black women, women like me, are still incarcerated at **twice the rate** of white women.

Behind every statistic is a name.
A story.
A daughter.
A mother.

Behind every number is a woman who needed help, not handcuffs.

I began journaling again, writing about everything I saw: the pain, the injustice, the sisterhood, and the hope that refused to die inside those walls. I started mentoring younger women, telling them, "You are not what you've done. You are what you survive."

It was in that cold dorm room, surrounded by women society had forgotten, that I made a promise to myself:

When I got out this time, I wouldn't just walk free. I would make freedom possible for others.

I didn't know how yet.
But I knew why.

That was the beginning of my healing.
That was the birth of my purpose.
That was the rise inside.

Looking back, I realize what I survived was never just personal, it was systemic. The bars that held me weren't only made of steel. They were built from policies, prejudice, and the silence of people who didn't believe women like me were redeemable.

I was a statistic before I was ever given space to be a story.

But Grace had other plans.

The revolving door that tried to claim me became the very thing that fueled my calling. I made a vow that no woman coming home after incarceration should ever have to walk blind into a world unprepared to receive her. No mother should have to choose between her freedom and her family, between survival and stability.

I was once that woman, shackled, scared, and told redemption was out of reach.

But now I know the truth: **we are never beyond restoration.** My story didn't end in those mountains.

It was born there.

CHAPTER 9

Beauty After the Bars: The Movement

When I came home the second time, I wasn't the same woman the system had tried to break.

I was done being quiet. I was done asking for permission to exist.

They called me "formerly incarcerated," but the truth was, I had been **formerly invisible**.

This time, I came home with a mission.

The streets I once walked looked different, but the struggle hadn't changed. Mothers were still trying to feed their babies. Families were still being torn apart by the system. Women were still carrying the weight of mistakes they had already paid for.

So I made myself a promise:

If nobody builds the bridge, I will.

And that's exactly what I did.

I had a vision in my head, but I didn't yet know where to start.

It was the 90s, and back then, reentry wasn't friendly. There were no roadmaps. No welcome mats. No systems built to catch you when you came home. Just locked doors, side-eyes, and a world that expected you to disappear quietly after you had paid your debt.

So I did what I've always done when the path wasn't clear—I started searching.

I researched. I listened. I learned. And slowly, I began to discover a movement rising from the ashes of mass incarceration—powerful freedom fighters who refused to let our people be erased. Women and men like Andrea James, Amy Povah, Fox Rich, Rita Gray, Celeste Wells, Kara Lee Nelson, Deanna Hoskins, Nkechi Tafia, Dee Rainer, Charlotte Garnes, Dr. Zaria Davis, Pamela Winn , Kemba Pradia Smith, Topeka K. Sam, Susan Burton, Kristie Puckett, Nicole Davis, Justin Moore, Virginia Douglas, Sharon Turner, Syrita Steib, Ruby Welch, Tia Hamilton, Sunshine Williams (NYC), Tiheba Baines, Nerika Jenkins, Donna Hylton, Tyra Imani Patterson, Big Shay Smith, Tray "Rock "Johns, Toni Willis, Danielle Metz, Keeda Haynes, Dawn Harrington, #FreeMichelleWest and Miquelle West- Ramona Brant and Grandma Phyllis Hardy, both Angels in Heaven-and so many more.

They didn't just talk about justice.

They built it. Abolished and burnt down injustices,

With their lives. With their scars. With their courage.

Watching them, studying them, learning from their journeys lit something in me. I realized I wasn't alone in this fire. There was a whole tribe of people saying, *We are more than our worst mistakes.*

And that's when I made myself a promise:

If nobody builds the bridge, I will.

And that's exactly what I did.

Beauty After the Bars was born—first in my journal, then in my spirit, and finally in the world. What started as a whisper between prison walls became a movement of safe homes, workforce programs, peer-support networks, and healing spaces for women coming home.

We didn't wait for permission.

We didn't wait for policy.

We started where we were, with what we had, and with who we loved.

Every woman we helped, every door and home we opened, every mother reunited with her child—all of it was an act of rebellion against a system that profits from our pain.

I told my team,

"We're not running a program. We're building a movement."

And we do! I worked tirelessly, sun up to sun down- often using my own funding- until I was gifted with grants or private donations.

The movement grew—first local, then statewide, and before long, national. We partnered with churches, nonprofits, justice agencies, and foundations that still believed in mercy. We held rallies and vigils, policy roundtables and prayer circles.

I stand in rooms with mayors, commissioners, and chiefs and told them straight:

"The women you forgot are coming home—and they're coming with purpose."

Some people didn't know how to handle me- and still don't and that is okay.

They wanted polished stories and safe conversations, not truth wrapped in scars and scripture. They wanted statistics, not testimonies. They wanted silence, not survival stories.

But I didn't come to make them comfortable.

I came to make change inevitable.

CHAPTER 10

The Movement Continues

Every other year, we honor that legacy at the Beauty After the Bars Fundraising Gala, a night of light, music, and purpose. It's not a red-carpet show; it's a sacred roll call for freedom.

During the Gala, we present two awards named after the women whose courage helped build this foundation: the **Ramona Brant Courage Award** and the **Phyllis "Grandma" Hardy Legacy Award**.

Before naming those awards, I reached out personally to both families, because respect is the foundation of everything we build. Their blessing mattered. Their voices mattered. Their stories mattered.

Those awards remind us, and the world, that we do this work not to make a dollar, but to make a difference.

Every ticket sold, every speech shared, every tear that falls in that room fuels another Safe Home, another job placement, another mother reunited with her child, another woman granted a second chance.

We travel city to city, state to state, and sometimes across borders, carrying our message to anyone who will listen:

Incarcerated women are not disposable.

We speak in churches, courthouses, community centers, and college classrooms.
We sit on panels beside lawmakers and sit on porches beside mothers still waiting on their daughters to come home.

Wherever we go, we bring the same fire that was born inside those prison walls.
We bring the same truth that saved us.
The same spirit of survival, sisterhood, and unshakeable hope.

Because this isn't charity.
This is change.
This is restoration.
This is redemption in motion.

And when we rise together, we remind the world exactly who we are:

Unbreakable.

THE FIRE

...

CHAPTER 11

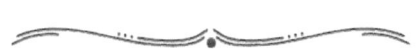

From the Projects to The People's Champ

I never planned to run for office.
In fact, when the idea first came to me, I said no, and I said it loud.

My plan was simple: keep meeting people where they were, serving, helping, and showing up in the community just like I always had. I had found my rhythm in the work, organizing food drives, mentoring women, mentoring in jail and prisons, opening safe Homes, marching, protesting, and standing shoulder-to-shoulder with my people on the front lines. I ran as The People's Champ long before politics ever entered the conversation. It wasn't a slogan. It was who I was.

But purpose doesn't ask for permission.
Purpose pushes you.

Every time I stood at a microphone talking about justice, I could feel something rising in me. For years, I knocked on doors asking people to vote for others, registering voters, and encouraging civic engagement. But I never saw myself as a politician. I could never put politics over people.

A girl from Southside Homes?
A woman who had once been a federal inmate?
Sitting on Charlotte City Council?

But then I remembered, those were the exact reasons I needed to run.

I looked around District 3 and saw the same struggles I grew up with. I've lived in this district for more than fifty years, and much of my family still does. The neighborhoods I loved were being transformed by development without inclusion. People were being displaced in the name of "progress."

I thought of the women in our Safe Homes trying to get bus passes, IDs, childcare, and jobs while the city talked about everything except them.

My community didn't need another politician.
They needed a representative.

They needed me.
They needed The People's Champ.

The Fight to Represent the People

In 2022, I ran in a special election and lost by just a few hundred votes to a well qualified, well-funded and smart incumbent. That loss didn't break me, it built me. Sometimes purpose has to go through process.

So when the seat opened again in 2023, I ran.
This time, I had two opponents, and one of those campaigns came with attacks that cut deep.

A mailer went out across District 3 asking:

"Do you know you have a habitual felon on the ballot?"

It was a public attempt to shame me for my past and discredit the very redemption that had transformed my life. But what they didn't understand was simple:

I wasn't the woman they tried to describe.
I had been home for decades.
My record didn't define me, my resurrection did.

My campaign wasn't fancy. There were no big donors or polished consultants. It was neighbors knocking on doors. Mothers making calls after work. Young justice impacted people registering to vote because, for the first time, they saw someone who looked like them, talked like them, and represented them.

We turned community hope into strategy, and movement into momentum.

When the early votes came in, precinct by precinct, we won every single one in District 3.

For the first time in Charlotte's history, a justice-impacted woman was elected to City Council.

District 3 spoke loud.
The people's seat finally belonged to one of the people.

The People's Seat

I earned every major endorsement, SEIU, the Metrolina Labor Council, the Black Political Caucus, the Charlotte Observer, the Meck Dems, and more. The city critics said I was the longshot, but the people said otherwise.

When I walked into City Hall for the first time, I carried every woman who ever wrote me from a prison cell, every child who had waited on their mother to come home, every grandmother who whispered, "Baby, don't let them forget about us."

So when I sit in that chamber, I don't vote with the elite.
I vote with the people.

I've stood my ground and voted no on issues that made national headlines. Critics accused me of "moving the city to the left." Whatever that means.

If voting with the people, calling out injustice, and making good trouble makes me "too far left," then I'll proudly wear that title, right beside The People's Champ.

I'm not being bought, sold, or told.
I remember exactly who sent me there, the mothers, the workers, the dreamers, the fighters still waiting for the world to see them.

The Weight and the Worth

Some days are still hard.
The lights are bright.
The politics are heavy.
The critics are loud.

But I stay grounded in the same truth that carried me through the gates of Alderson and brought me home:

I wasn't chosen because I was perfect.
I was chosen because I'm proof.

Every time I cast a vote, I think of Southside Homes, the place that raised me. The people who believed in me when society didn't. I think of my Mama, Grandma Lula, my sister, my aunts, my cousins, my daughters and the Legacy of this movement -Ramona Brant, Phyllis "Grandma" Hardy, the women who fought battles in private so I could fight mine in public.

Being The People's Champ isn't a title.
It's a calling.

It means speaking truth even when it shakes rooms.
Standing firm when others fold.

Loving your community so deeply that you refuse to abandon it, no matter how high you climb.

From the projects to City Hall, my story isn't just about survival. It's about stewardship.

It's about what happens when a woman the world counted out decides to count herself in.

I may have started behind bars, but I rose to break them, not just for me, but for every woman, every child, every forgotten soul who dares to believe that redemption is real.

Because titles fade.

Elections pass.

But the work, the people's work, endures.

And that's why they call me **The People's Champ.**

CHAPTER 12

The Fire Inside City Hall

When the noise gets loud and the weight feels heavy, I remind myself who I am, and *whose* I am.

When some of my colleagues tried to make me feel like I didn't belong at the dais, I often reminded them that I won every precinct.- (something that has only been achieved by me).

The people put me in this seat, and only the people can remove me.

I knew I wasn't their typical councilwoman. I didn't come from wealth. I didn't come from political legacy. And I didn't walk in with a last name that opened doors.

But I held my head high and carried my dignity everywhere I went. I reminded folks often: I won just like they won, but I made history while doing it. What I accomplished had never been done in the history of Charlotte City Council:

Winning every single precinct- confirmation that I earned the right to be in City Hall

There was one colleague who used his longevity, privilege and tenure to try to intimidate me. But intimidation never worked on me, it always backfired. I spoke my truth boldly, directly, and unapologetically. If I had been weak, I would've quit a long time ago. But there is absolutely nothing weak about me.

I've survived darker nights than politics.
I've stood before judges.
I've faced critics.
I've watched headlines twist my story.

And yet, I am still standing.

Every morning before stepping into City Hall, I remind myself that God sent me here.

So tell me, how are you going to top God?

I turn on my gospel music, let the lyrics wash over me, and I pray without ceasing:

"God, guide my heart and guard my mouth. Let me lead with purpose, not pride."

That prayer keeps me steady when the spotlight burns too hot. My faith reminds me that favor doesn't fade just because people do. My family reminds me that love is louder than lies. And my community reminds me that leadership is service, not status.

Grace in the Halls

City Hall will test you.

People judge you by what you wear, who you speak to, who you call your friends and what you post on social media. The work will stretch you. The politics will try to shake you. The pressure will push you toward breaking points if you let it.

But I've already walked through fires hotter than this, and I came out refined, not reduced.

There were days I'd greet people in the hallway and they wouldn't even look my way. Elevator rides were their own kind of comedy, folks would step in without speaking and step out the same way.

Classless.

But I'd smile inside because I knew exactly where I was headed, to the 15th floor, where the Mayor, the City Manager, and the City Council offices were. And every day I reminded myself: Councilmember Brown has an office on the 15th floor.

I belong here. I was chosen by the people.

I came in dressed to impress, makeup flawless, hair laid, nails polished. Not because I thought I was better than anyone else, but because I knew I was just as good.

I spoke to everyone, the security guards who kept us safe, the staff who delivered our council packets, the people who cleaned the building, the cafeteria workers who greeted us with warmth. Not a single day went by where I didn't bring sunshine into those halls.

I reminded the Constituent Services staff on a daily and consistent basis- that we were a team, and that they were a vital part of it. "We're in this together," I told them often. They told me how much I meant to them, and I always sent that love and gratitude right back.

I met with community members, leaders, and developers every week, and I heard the same thing over and over again:

"I've never been in the City Council offices before."

That broke my heart and fueled my purpose. My constituents deserved to know I was human, accessible, real, and present. I often answered my own emails, helped my staff, and treated everyone with dignity. I didn't just show up for the community after I won, I had been showing up long before.

I remember a candidate running against me once saying something foolish like, "Why do you meet so many people in your office?"

My answer was simple:

"Because the taxpayers pay for it- so we should use it. The council exists for the constituents to use it and for council business.

I constantly reminded my colleagues that these seats don't belong to us, they belong to the people.

And behind those closed doors, I saw a lot.
Politics can be dirty.
People lie, plot, and do anything for power.

But I never let that change me. I was the same leader committed to the people and my community- day after day. Meeting after meeting. I did not let politics change me.

Unbreakable Purpose

City Hall was never supposed to be comfortable for someone like me, and that's exactly why I belonged there. I carried the voices of people who never had a seat at the table and made sure they were finally heard.

No matter what storm comes, I walk through those glass doors every day with my head high and my heart steady.

Because I wasn't chosen by chance.
I was chosen by purpose.

The fire didn't burn me down.
It built me up.

And I'm still here, **unbreakable**.

CHAPTER 13

When the Fire Turned on Me

When the allegations came out, everything changed.

People I had stood beside, people who once called me for every event, every photo, every issue that needed "the people's voice", suddenly went silent. The same folks who once needed my strength and my name began to distance themselves. They didn't call. They didn't check in. They didn't even ask if I was okay.

And I noticed.

Many elected officials, I won't call their names, because they know exactly who they are, quietly pulled away. The silence was loud. The distance was deliberate.

WHEN - the allegations came out -I never heard a single word from the Mayor. Someone I once respected, supported, and believed in put so much distance between us that it spoke louder than any press statement ever could. Council was already under fire for transparency issues, that's public record, and when my allegations hit the headlines, it was almost as if my pain became their protection.

My storm became their cover.

I was deeply disappointed in the way some of my colleagues handled it.

I won't lie—I was disappointed that the Mayor never checked on me.

In a moment when the fire was hottest and the smoke was everywhere, silence spoke louder than words. But I also learned something just as important: who did stand with me. And to those people, they know exactly who they are. I will forever honor them.

One name I will say out loud is Councilmember Johnson. She was the only member of City Council who reached out to me the very day the allegations hit the public media. That mattered. In moments like that, you don't forget who shows up.

I have my receipts.

As I wrote this book, I went back to the calls and the texts, to the timestamps and the messages, to see who reached for me on the actual day of the fire and the smoke. Not for politics. Not for appearances. But for humanity.

History records who speaks when it's safe.

But I remember who spoke when it wasn't.

They checked on me. They made sure I knew I wasn't alone.
That mattered more than they'll ever know.

If you are wondering if you are in public service or not- check your receipts- I got mines!

Because truthfully, I showed up for everyone. I never cared about party lines or titles. If there was a need, I was there. I spent my time in office fighting for justice, housing, equity, and community, not politics. And when the storm came, I expected at least a fraction of that same grace back.

But grace isn't something everyone gives when the cameras start rolling.

Standing in the Fire

The same week the smear hit the news, I had a Town Hall in Steele Creek, one of the most important communities in District 3. The audience that night was predominantly white, but the warmth in that room was undeniable.

It turned out to be one of the best Town Halls I've ever hosted.

Not one person asked about the allegations.
Not one.

They came to talk about real issues, housing, public safety, development. And when the media slid in at the end, trying to stir something up, the residents spoke before I even could.

"Let her have her day in court."
"At least she showed up."
"I didn't think she would come, but she did."

That moment reminded me exactly why I do this work. Because leadership isn't about hiding when it's hard, it's about showing up anyway.

What made that night even more telling was this: several elected officials had been scheduled to attend that Town Hall.

Not one of them showed up.
Not. One.- if it was truly about the work they would have attended- but the Fire was to hot for them- in my opinion they abandoned me and the people that voted for them.

They were quick to stand beside me when the cameras were flashing, but when the fire came, they vanished. I stood alone, and yet, surrounded by my people, I felt stronger than ever.

The Trial by Media

The media was a whole different tornado.
They smeared the hell out of me, and they did it repeatedly. Every time my name appeared, it was:

"Indicted Councilmember."

Not *Councilmember Brown*.
Not *Dr. Tiawana Brown*.
Just that label, repeated like a drumbeat meant to destroy me.

It wasn't reporting.
It was **reputation assassination**.

And deep down, I knew this: if I wasn't Black, the coverage wouldn't have been so heavy, so relentless, or so eager. They didn't simply report the story, they tried me in the media before I ever had my day in court.

And in my opinion, that trial by media played a huge role in the outcome of my re-election.

They showed up everywhere:
At my court appearances.
At my election filing.
At my community events.

Over and over, they showed up, hoping I'd break.

They drilled me, cornered me, and crafted whatever narrative suited them. They thought the pressure would make me resign.

But they underestimated me.

I've faced judges.
I've faced iron gates.
I've survived storms that would've buried most people.

A headline wasn't going to make me surrender.

When people tweeted that I was "arrogant" for not stepping down, I laughed. Because opinions are like assholes, everybody's got one.

And when the chatter in City Hall got loud, I reminded them of a simple truth:

"If it weren't for my headline, some of y'all would still be under fire. You had issues before I came to Council, and you'll have issues after I'm gone."

That wasn't arrogance, that was accountability.

I still think it's ridiculous that I made national news because Charlotte's local outlets made the story national. They amplified my pain for clicks and ratings, proving yet again how quickly the world profits off a Black woman's downfall.

But what broke my heart most wasn't how they treated *me*, it was how they came for my family.

The online hate was vicious.

My daughters became targets of cruelty, racism, and judgment. My family worried about safety everywhere we went- (this was because of the heavy media coverage)

And in the middle of all of it, my daughters—Antoinette and Tijema—became nameless.

To the world, they were no longer two grown women with their own lives, their own dreams, their own worth. They became reduced to a headline: "Councilmember Brown and her daughters." Their names, their value, their substance were stripped away by a media narrative that tried to make them faceless and interchangeable.

But their names matter.

Their lives matter.

Their stories matter.

My daughters didn't ask for this. They didn't deserve to have their peace stolen or their names dragged through the mud for something they had nothing to do with. They didn't sign up for public office. I did.

Watching them carry that weight was one of the hardest parts of this journey.

But even in that pain, I reminded them:

You are more than a headline.

You are more than someone else's story.

You are not defined by this moment.

Your names still carry power, purpose, and promise.

Storms don't last forever.

Even so-called friends will stay so-called friends when the storm passes. And it *will* pass.

Because Scripture told me long before any headline did:

"Weeping may endure for a night, but joy comes in the morning."
— Psalm 30:5

So I stood tall — rooted in faith, unshaken by fear.
I didn't run from the fire, **I stood in it**.

Because I knew my truth.
I knew my God.
And I knew this storm wouldn't have the final say.

And when the smoke cleared, I was still standing —
Scarred but stronger.
Tested but triumphant.
Unbroken and unbowed.

I come from a long line of strong Black women, and during my most challenging moments, I could feel every ounce of their strength moving through me.

That's how I made it through.
That's how I kept going.

THE FIGHT

...

CHAPTER 14

Faith, Family and; Forward

When the world starts spinning too fast, I go back to my foundation, faith and family.

They are the reason I keep showing up when everything in me wants to hide.

They are the quiet strength behind the public fight.

My mother, **Artie Mae Brown,** is the anchor of my life. Her prayers have covered me more times than I can count. I am who I am because she never stopped believing I could rise again. She is the definition of unconditional love, the kind that doesn't shake when the world turns its back.

My daughters, **Antoinette and Tijema,** are the pieces of my heart that walk this earth.
They've seen me at my strongest and my weakest, yet they still call me "Mom" with pride. They have stood beside me through storms most people couldn't imagine, and watching them grow into mothers, leaders, and women of their own strength has been my greatest reward.

And then there's my grandson, **Byron Jr.** — my pure joy.
His laughter is medicine.
His hugs are peace.
Every time he runs into my arms, I see proof that generational curses can be broken and blessings can begin again.

My sister, **Chunta**, is my best friend — my peace in human form. She listens when the noise gets too loud, tells me the truth even when it stings, and reminds me that all my good outweighs any mistake. She's the shoulder I lean on, the voice of reason when my heart feels heavy, and the one who brings me back to center every single time.

My Aunt **Valare** is my prayer partner and spiritual warrior.
When I say we pray, I mean we *pray*.
She reminds me that God is real, His promises never return void, and the storms we face aren't meant to destroy us — they're meant to reveal our strength. When trouble comes, she's right there praying with me, listening to my cries, and standing with me, and reminding me that faith without fear is how we win.

Cousin Barbara Phillips, who grew up more like an aunt to me, has been a steady anchor in my life. Every day, without fail, we share prayers and affirmations through simple text messages. In the middle of chaos, her words come gently but powerfully—reminding me that forgiveness is what God calls us to, and that no storm lasts forever. When my faith feels heavy, her messages lift it, whispering hope into my spirit and assuring me that this too shall pass.

And then there's my cousin **Peewee** — the cousin who became my sister.

We grew up side by side, sharing rooms, food, and dreams. She's family by blood but sister by choice, one of the constants who has walked every season with me, from Southside Homes to City Hall. Peewee's loyalty is rare, her love is solid, and her presence in my life proves that real family isn't just given, it's chosen and earned.

These women — my mother, my daughters, my sister, my aunt, and my cousins, are my **living circle of strength.**
They hold me accountable, keep me grounded, and remind me daily that my purpose didn't come easy, it came honestly. They are the ones who keep my faith burning when I'm tired, who remind me that grace is bigger than guilt, and who never let me forget that I'm covered, by love, by prayer, and by purpose.

Faith and family keep me steady when success tries to lift me too high and criticism tries to pull me too low. They remind me to be human first, humble always, and hopeful no matter what.

Every prayer whispered by my mother…
Every hug from my daughters…
Every smile from Byron Jr.…
Every late-night talk with my sister…
Every call with Peewee…
Every prayer circle with my aunt and cousins…

All of it builds the woman I continue to become.

So when I walk into City Hall, I don't walk in alone.
I walk in carrying their love, their faith, and their prayers.

Tiawana Brown

They are my roots.
They are my reason.
They are my forever.

CHAPTER 15

The Heartbeat of City Hall

Where Humanity Meets Leadership

The Office of Constituent Services is the bridge between the people and their government in Charlotte, North Carolina. It is where compassion meets policy, where the cries, questions, and concerns of residents become real solutions. This office supports the Mayor, City Council, and city departments by listening, responding, and making sure every voice is heard.

It is the quiet heartbeat that keeps City Hall connected to the people it serves, steady, consistent, and powerful.

They are not "the help."
They are mothers, daughters, sisters, aunts, fathers, and sons.
They are human beings.

And from day one, that is exactly how I treated every single one of them.

I came into City Hall humble, grounded in gratitude, and ready to serve. It was easy for me to treat them as colleagues because I know what it feels like to be judged by labels instead of character. As a justice-impacted woman, I've spent my life reclaiming dignity, my own and others'. I've learned that every person deserves humanity, and restoring it is not just work for me.

It's ministry.

City Hall didn't change that, it expanded it.

Inside those walls, I saw my own spirit reflected in the incredible individuals who make up Constituent Services. They are not support staff; they are partners in purpose. They are the pulse of City Hall, the ones who keep the engine of government moving with integrity, compassion, professionalism, and patience.

Public service is never a one-person job.
It takes a village.

And that village lives in the hallways of City Hall, where love meets leadership, where teamwork meets purpose, and where dignity is restored in everyday moments.

My Village in City Hall

Amanda — your leadership is the heartbeat of the team. You love everyone and treat us all the same — with fairness, compassion, and grace. You lead with a calm strength that kept us grounded.

Jacquelyn — you are the face of Constituent Services. Your prayers, your kindness, your spirit of light radiate far beyond City Hall. Your presence proves that hope still lives in public service.

Antawuan — the big brother of the team. Surrounded by women yet always standing tall with protection and patience. Your instinct is to shield, support, and uplift. Thank you for being our anchor and voice of reason.

LaToya — your work ethic is unmatched. Dependable, hardworking, radiant — like a rainbow after the storm. You always kept me informed and steady.

Natasha — though you were the newest member, you came in ready. You stepped right into your role, spread your wings, and flew. Assigned to me personally, you adapted to my work style with ease, grace, and excellence. Together, we made it work.

Kristy — my young leader. You are pure light. I smile every time I think of you. You greeted me with joy every single day, and it meant the world. You showed me what it looks like to lead with positivity and purpose.

Alexis- you are easy like Sunday morning. And even though our paths didn't cross as often as some, every time you came around, I could feel the warmth of your spirit and the quiet power of your positive affirmations. Your presence spoke without words—gentle, calming, and full of light—and it left an imprint on me that I will always carry.

Jocella — my twin. Same height, same energy, same vibe. So many days we walked into City Hall unintentionally matching, like the universe was in on the joke. You reminded me that Black girls rock, that authenticity is a superpower, and that joy itself is an act of resistance. In moments when I needed it most, you reflected back to me the strength I carry and the power I hold, reminding me that the people still need my voice.

Alonna — I could never leave you out. You took care of business and handled every task with confidence. You kept everything running smoothly. I missed you when you left, but I'll always be grateful that you started this journey with me.

Each of you showed me what real integrity in public service looks like, teamwork, patience, grace, and heart. You are the quiet strength behind the scenes, the glue that holds City Hall together.

"Thank you" will never be enough, but it will always be sincere.

City Hall taught me that restoring dignity doesn't stop at policy.
It lives in every smile.
Every act of patience.
Every unseen moment of grace.

Closing Reflection

City Hall was more than a building, it was a proving ground for grace under pressure.

Inside those walls, I learned that leadership isn't just about showing up in meetings; it's about showing up for people. I learned that love can live inside bureaucracy, that faith can survive under fluorescent lights, and that dignity can still breathe in government.

Yet even as I served with my whole heart, storms gathered outside those doors.
The same compassion that made me a bridge for the people also made me a target for politics.

But as I would soon learn, even when the fire comes, the heartbeat doesn't stop.
It only grows stronger.

Author's Reflection

"Unbreakable: The Rise, The Fire, and The Fight – Part One"

When I sat down to write this book, I didn't want to tell a pretty story. I wanted to tell the truth.

Not the kind that plays well on a stage or sounds good on a panel, but the kind that costs you something.

The kind born from being counted out, misunderstood, overlooked, and still showing up.
The kind that takes a woman from the system to the seat, from brokenness to boldness,
from surviving to serving.

I am not supposed to be here, but purpose overrules statistics every single time.

Every page of this book is a testimony to grace, grit, and God.
I wrote it for every justice-impacted soul who ever believed their story was too heavy for healing,
too messy for redemption,
too complicated to be seen,
too painful to be understood.

I wrote this for everyone who has ever faced the justice system and fought to be seen as more than a number. For every person who stood tall inside a federal prison. For every spirit still struggling to be heard. For every human being who needed a second chance… and then another.

I wrote this for every person who has lived through trauma.
For the unhoused, who learned how to survive without safety.
For every domestic violence survivor who found the courage to leave and the strength to live.
For Black women in leadership and positions of power, justice impacted elected officials and those elected officials that are not, for those of us carrying both the crown and the cross.
For those battling mental health challenges in a world that too often looks away.
For every child born into poverty who was made to believe their circumstances were their destiny.

This is for anyone who was ever told—by systems, by statistics, by silence—that you can't become.

I wrote this for the ones who were underestimated, overlooked, and written off. For those who kept dreaming when all the evidence said they shouldn't. For the fighters. For the builders. For the bridge-makers.

I wrote it for the mothers.
The daughters.
The fighters.
The forgotten.
The ones who rise anyway.

I walked through fire, but I didn't burn.
I built from ashes and stood in the very halls that once would've denied me entry.
And when I got there, I didn't shrink,
I shined.

This is only **Part One** — The rise.

The fire is still to come.
And when it does, I won't whisper.

I'll roar.

Because I am **Unbreakable**.
And so are you. -this book is for you.

— **Tiawana Brown**
The People's Champ
"When We Fight, We Win."

Epilogue

"The Rise Continues"

The lights dim, the meetings end, and the voices fade, but purpose doesn't clock out.

When I walk out of City Hall and into the quiet, I carry every name, every story, and every soul I've ever fought for.

This journey was never about a title.
It was about trust, trust from the people who believed, trust from the women who called me sister, trust from the ones who looked at me and saw hope instead of history.

I've learned that healing doesn't always happen in silence.
Sometimes, it happens in **service**.

And even though I've been bruised by systems and scarred by struggle, I remain devoted to love, radical, unshakable, resilient love.

The rise has been beautiful, but it came with lessons only fire could teach.
Even when the world tried to dim my light,
I learned how to glow from within.

So to everyone still rising, still hoping, still rebuilding, **hold on.**

Because the story doesn't end here.

The next chapter begins where courage meets confrontation and *Unbreakable* becomes more than a title.

It becomes a **testimony**.

And when that next season comes, I will stand not just as a woman who survived, but as **Councilmember Brown — The People's Champ —** proof that redemption walks, speaks, and leads with power… and that no system can silence a soul that has already been set free.

About Author

Councilmember **Tiawana Brown** is a trailblazing public servant, justice-impacted leader, motivational speaker, and storyteller whose journey from generational poverty to incarceration to elected office has inspired audiences across the nation. She is the founder of *Beauty After the Bars*, a nonprofit dedicated to empowering women and families through wrap around services that meet you on the inside of a prison or jail cell- to provide safe homes, full wrap around services, peer support, and second-chance opportunities. Its mission is to support women both inside and outside of jail and prison while interrupting the incarceration of women and girls through advocacy, education, and community care.

Born and raised in Charlotte, North Carolina, Tiawana learned early the meaning of faith, perseverance, and unconditional love from her hardworking single mother, **Artie Mae Brown**. She made history as the first justice-impacted person ever elected to the Charlotte City Council, in the 14th largest city in the United States.

Her life is one of resilience and redemption. From her humble beginnings in Charlotte's Southside Homes housing projects, now under the umbrella of Inlivian, to surviving domestic violence and recidivism, Tiawana transformed her pain into purpose and her story into a movement. While serving a federal prison sentence more than three decades ago, she gave birth to her youngest daughter, **Tijema**, an experience that would later fuel her mission to fight for women, families, and second chances. Her incarceration became the spark that ignited her purpose, turning pain into power and lived experience into a lifelong commitment to justice and restoration.

Over the years, she has been honored with numerous awards and recognitions for her leadership, community service, and commitment to justice reform. As a national motivational speaker and storyteller, she travels the country sharing her message of hope, faith, and transformation, proving that your past does not define your purpose.

As the founder of the *District 3 Community Coalition*, she continues to serve beyond elected office, building bridges between residents, advocates, and organizations committed to healing and transformation.

A proud mother of two adult daughters — **Antionette and Tijema**, and grandmother to her beloved grandson, **Byron Bernard Sadler, Jr. (BJ)**, Tiawana's life and leadership reflect her unwavering belief in faith, family, and second chances. She is a devoted member of Greater Mount Sinai Baptist Church, located in the heart of District 3's Historic West Side, where her faith remains the foundation of her purpose.

Tiawana is also an honor student at Johnson C. Smith University (JCSU), pursuing a degree in Criminal Justice and continuing her lifelong commitment to learning, leadership, and service.

Her debut memoir, *Unbreakable: The Rise, The Fire, and The Fight – Part One*, captures her remarkable journey from the federal prison system to elected office, a testimony of grace, grit, and God's power to turn pain into purpose.

Known to many as **"The People's Champ,"** Tiawana lives by her creed:

"When we fight, we win."

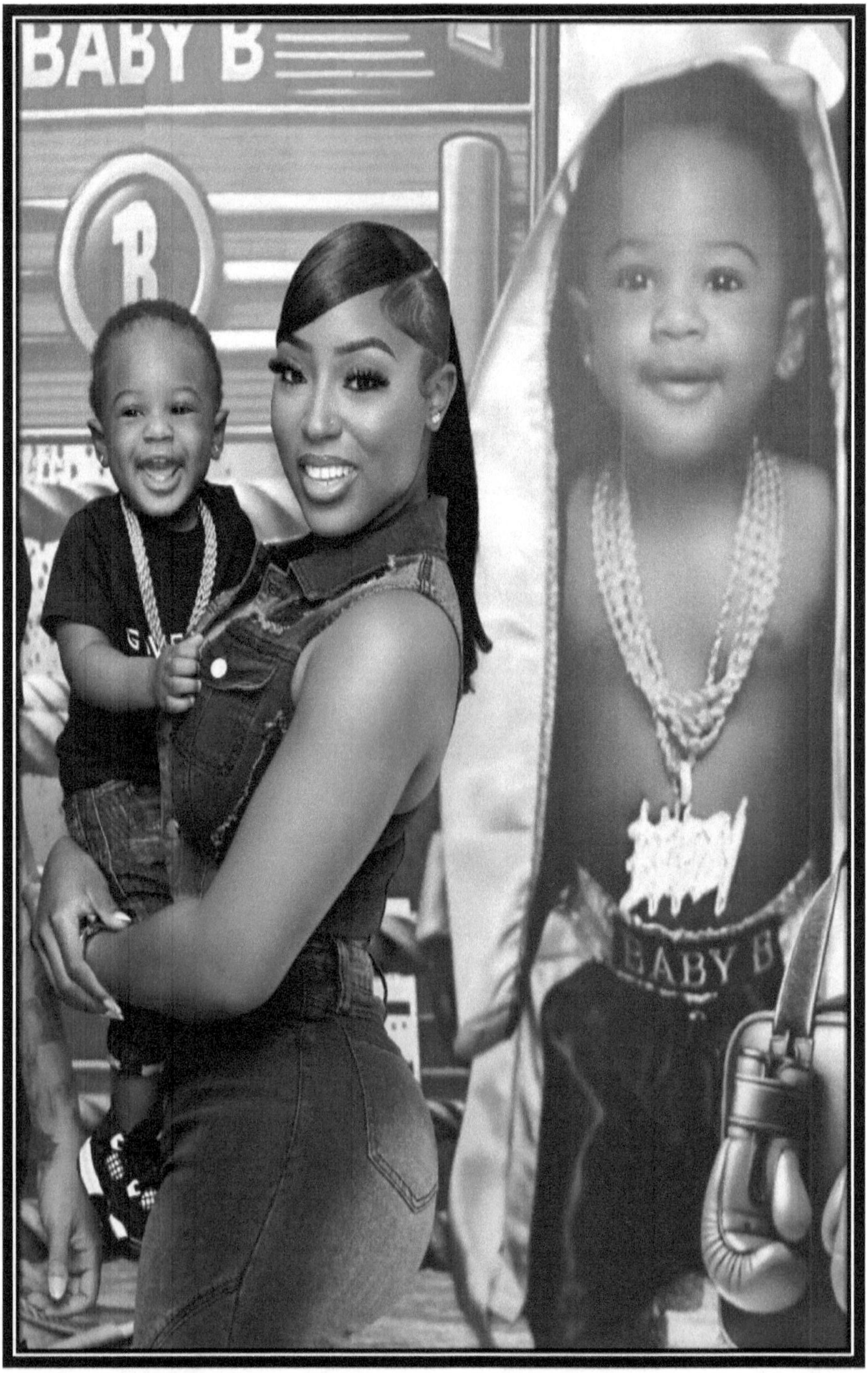
BABY B
BABY B

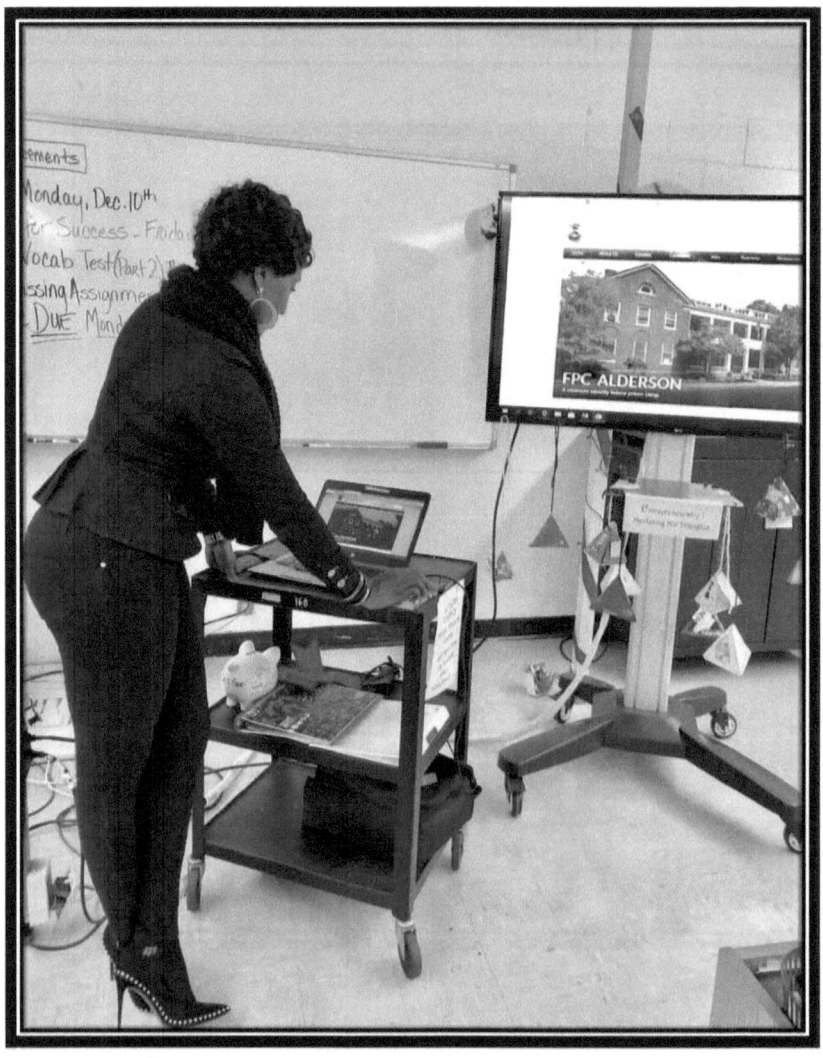

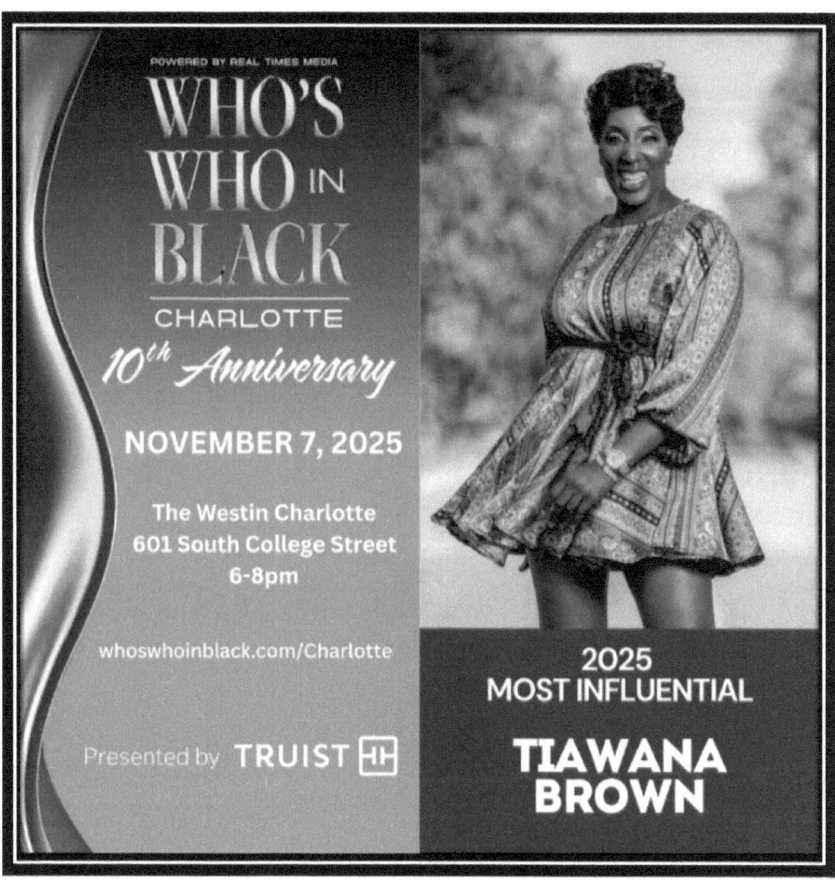

Special Thanks

To my KNL softball teammates, coaches and staff- BSA Softball, and USSA- Softball life is the best stress relief.

To University of North Carolina at Chapel Hill, Megan Foster, and the incredible cast of students who brought the Fight Like Hell stage play to life—thank you.

Your performance was nothing short of extraordinary. You carried truth, pain, courage, and resilience across that stage with such care and conviction. A special and deeply personal shout-out to the student who portrayed me—who embodied my fight with such authenticity—while I was literally fighting like hell in real time, and none of you even knew. That moment will stay with me forever.

To the Emmy Award-winning documentary team—Erica, Joseph, and the entire staff—thank you for thinking enough of me to include my story. Your work honors lived experience, elevates truth, and ensures that voices like mine are not erased, minimized, or forgotten.

All of you are the real MVPs.
Your artistry, courage, and commitment to telling hard stories with integrity matter more than you know.

Thank You For Your Support

Ace-(DJ Ace,) Adolph R. Shiver, Alaina Sweasy, Alfron Patterson, Almetra Jones, Angela Buford Hayes, Andrea Hudson, Andrew Benton Gilliard-("Nomo Buster"), Angela Chambers, Anthony Morrow, Anthony Hines, Antoine Hamilton, Antonio D. Thomas, Big Murphyz, Big Pervis -(Sin City,) Brandi williams, Chewy- (iamchewy5), Camilla Ervin, Carla A. Carlisle, Charlotte Garnes, Cheryl Miller, Colin Graham, Crystal Neal, Curtis Hayes Jr, Damion Robinson, David Mensah *(best trainer ever)*, Debra Bennett- Austin, Dedra Allen, Demarco Cheerboy Dawson, Denise Coleman, Donell "Dink" Gardner, Donna Belk, Dorothy Marie Gaines, Dr. Gregory Burks, Dr. Zaria Davis, Eric-Amir Shabazz, Greg Walker, Ian Miller, Kerwin Pittman, Kristie & Elevator Jay, Liliana Maria, Mikki Watson & Jerome- (Radio One), Mike Rhynes Jr, Ellis Hunter, Fonda Bryant, Jason Hernandez, Jessica McFadden, Jessica "Ms. Jessica"(power-98), Jenesia (Tee-Tee) & Sammy Shannon, Jennifer Jones, Jody K. Polk, Jonathan "Jugg" Dorset, Judge Mobley, Judge Newton, Judge Patterson-Wrighton, Judge Trosch, Juan Cuartas, JD Mazuera Arias, Kevin W. Poirier, Kia M. Long- Alston, Lakira Brown-Santos, Latrica Hunter, Malcolm Sanders, Monica Cooper, Mali Green, Malik King, Nadine Fraylon, Nejaun Johnson, Nicole Conway, Ohavia Phillips Reed, Ophelia Burnett, Otissa and Tonya Marble, Traletta Banks, Patrick D. Cannon, Pauline Rogers, Raymond Beamon, Raymont Gause, Rev. Michelle Simmons, Resha Fortson, Rhondra Simpson, Robin Michelle Massey, Robin Woods, Samantha Council, Shawn and Niya Kennedy, Star and Veronica *(Miami Butterfly Reunion 2023)*, Stacy Hamilton, Susan Mason, Tailor Made *(Melissa)*, Teresa (your husband), Jordyn, Wanda and Reggie *(best neighbors ever)*, Tee Gill & Ramon Gill, River Family, Tia Hamilton, Tiheba Bain, Tiffany Jordan, Tina Mackey, Tommy Nichols, Thomas "Tony" Williams, Tracey D. Syphax, Wanda Dupree, Warren and Candice Moffatt, Willie J Holley, Jr, Vinroy Reid, Yasmine Arrington Brooks.

To all of the Women and girls in Beauty after the Bars program- current and past- all of you are the center of my Joy and why I "Fight Like Hell"

www.ingramcontent.com/pod-product-compliance
Lightning Source LLC
Chambersburg PA
CBHW020739230426
43665CB00009B/494